Tsunamis

Titles in the Natural Disasters series include:

Natural **Disasters**

Tsunamis

Andrew A. Kling

LUCENT
BOOKS®

THOMSON
———— ✳ ————™
GALE

San Diego • Detroit • New York • San Francisco • Cleveland • New Haven, Conn. • Waterville, Maine • London • Munich

For more information, contact
Lucent Books
27500 Drake Rd.
Farmington Hills, MI 48331-3535
Or you can visit our Internet site at http://www.gale.com

LIBRARY OF CONGRESS CATALOGING-IN-PUBLICATION DATA

Kling, Andrew A., 1961–
     Tsunamis / by Andrew A. Kling.
     p. cm. — (Natural disasters)
     Summary: A detailed description of tsunamis which includes their causes as well as the
     prediction of their occurrence and techniques of survival and rescue afterwards.
     Includes bibliographical references and index.
         ISBN 1-59018-222-7 (hardback : alk. paper)
         1. Tsunamis—Juvenile literature. [1.Tsunamis.] I. Title. II. Natural disasters (Lucent
Books)
         GC221.5 .K57 2003
         551.47'024—dc21

                                                                                              2002008906

Printed in the United States of America

Contents

Foreword

Fear and fascination are the two most common human responses to nature's most devastating events. People fear the awesome force of an earthquake, a volcanic eruption, a hurricane, and other natural phenomena with good reason. An earthquake can reduce multistory buildings to rubble in a matter of seconds. A volcanic eruption can turn lush forests and glistening lakes into a gray, flat landscape of mud and ash. A hurricane can lift houses from their foundations and hurl trucks and steel beams through the air.

As one witness to Hurricane Andrew, which hit Florida in 1992, recounts: "After the storm, planks and pieces of plywood were found impaling the trunks of large palms. . . . Eighteen-foot-long steel and concrete tie beams with roofs still attached were carried more than 150 feet. Paint was peeled from walls and street signs were sucked out of the ground and hurled through houses. Flying diesel fuel drums were a hazard, as were signs, awnings, decks, trash barrels, and fence posts that filled the skies. Mobile homes not only blew apart during the storm but disintegrated into aluminum shrapnel that became embedded in surrounding structures."

Fear is an understandable response to an event such as this but it is not the only emotion people experience when caught in the throes of a natural disaster or when news of one blares from radios or flashes across television screens. Most people are fascinated by natural forces that have the power to claim life, crush homes, tear trees from their roots, and devastate whole communities—all in an instant. Why do such terrible events as these fascinate people? Perhaps the answer lies in humanity's inability to control them, and in the knowledge that they will recur—in some cases without warning—despite the scientific community's best efforts to understand and predict them.

A great deal of scientific study has been devoted to understanding and predicting natural phenomena such as earthquakes, volcanic eruptions, and hurricanes. Geologists and seismologists monitor the earth's motion from thousands of locations around the world. Their sensitive instruments record even the slightest shifts in the large tectonic plates that make up the earth's crust. Tools such as these have greatly improved efforts to predict natural disasters. When Mt. Pinatubo in the Philippines awoke from its six-hundred-year slumber in 1991, for example, a team of scientists armed with seismometers, tiltmeters, and personal computers successfully predicted when the volcano would explode.

Clearly, the scientific community has made great strides in knowledge and in the ability to monitor and even predict some of nature's most catastrophic events. Prediction techniques have not yet been perfected, however, and control of these events eludes humanity entirely. From the moment a tropical disturbance forms over the ocean, for example, researchers can track its progress and follow every twist in its path to becoming a hurricane but they cannot predict with certainty where it will make landfall. As one researcher writes: "No one knows when or where [a catastrophic hurricane] will strike, but we do know that eventually it will blast ashore somewhere and cause massive destruction. . . . Since there is nothing anyone can do to alter that foreboding reality, the question is: Are we ready for the next great hurricane?"

The many gaps in knowledge, coupled with the inability to control these events and the certainty that they will recur, may help explain humanity's continuing fascination with natural disasters. The Natural Disasters series provides clear and careful explanations, vivid examples, and the latest information about how and why these events occur, what efforts are being made to predict them, and to prepare for them. Annotated bibliographies provide readers with ideas for further research. Fully documented primary and secondary source quotations enliven the text. Each book in this series provides students with a wealth of information as well as launching points for further study.

Introduction

The Aegean Sea, Circa 1450 B.C.

Almost thirty-five hundred years ago, several huge walls of water, the largest perhaps fifty meters (160 feet) tall, slammed into the islands of Thera and Crete in the Aegean Sea. These waves, called tsunamis, resulted from the explosion of Thera's largest volcano and, some scientists believe, may have supplied the factual basis for one of the world's most famous legends.

The legend of the lost continent of Atlantis is both familiar and romantic. According to the stories of the Greek philosopher Plato, the continent was larger than Africa and Asia combined and was home to people who ruled over Africa "as far as Egypt, and over Europe as far as Tuscany."[1] Plato claims that on "one grievous day and night . . . the island of Atlantis . . . was swallowed up by the sea and vanished."[2] Recent geological and archaeological findings suggest that the source of Plato's tale was the disastrous series of tsunamis that struck Thera and Crete.

Thera and its larger neighbor Crete were once home to a culture archaeologists call the Minoans. The Minoans had flourished for over a thousand years, extending their influence across the Mediterranean and as far away as Egypt. But suddenly, about thirty-five hundred years ago, they were no longer mentioned in historical or business records.

The disappearance of the Minoans may be related to a period of intense eruptions from Thera's main volcano. Archaeologists and geologists theorize that the center, or caldera, of the volcano collapsed during a particularly violent eruption, causing as much as thirty-two square miles of land to vanish beneath the waves. After flooding the landscape surrounding the caldera, the seawater then crashed outward into the Aegean Sea. The waters

A view of the Aegean Sea island of Thera. Thera was partially destroyed by volcanic eruptions and tsunamis about thirty-five hundred years ago, wiping out the ancient Minoan civilization.

soon returned in the form of tsunamis, and waves that may have been up to fifty meters tall struck along the coasts of Thera and Crete, wiping out countless towns and villages—and, in turn, the Minoan culture.

Egyptian merchants realized early on that something terrible had happened in the Aegean. According to Greek author Spyridon Marinatos, "The Egyptians had unquestionably heard about the sinking of an island, which was Thera, but this island, small and insignificant, was unknown to them."[3] But the Egyptians did know Thera's neighbor, Crete, which had suffered great damage from the sea and with which Egypt had abruptly lost contact.

As the years passed and no Minoan traders returned to the great Egyptian port of Alexandria, the accounts of the catastrophe in the Aegean grew worse. By the time of Plato, more than a thousand years later, around 350 B.C., people shared tales of an ancient seafaring race, rulers of a huge island beyond the Mediterranean in the Atlantic Ocean, that had died out when the sea swallowed their island.

The ancient tsunamis that had wreaked such havoc on the Minoans today live on in the story of Atlantis. Atlantis may not have existed as Plato described it, but the forces that can cause the sea to swallow an island still exist. Tsunamis did not disappear with the Minoans; they are still a very real and ever-present threat for the earth's islands and coastlines.

What Is a Tsunami?

Tsunamis are unlike any other phenomenon on earth. They can be born in any body of water, such as a lake, an ocean, or a bay. They can develop quickly or take days to build. They can travel across an open ocean as fast as a commercial jet airplane can fly across it. They can strike with little or no warning, and can carry people, houses, and even ships several miles inland from the coast. Tsunamis have been around since before the dawn of humankind, and although human history has been recording them for over two thousand years, only now are scientists beginning to understand how tsunamis are formed, how they behave, and how we can prepare for them before they strike.

The Ancient "Harbor Waves" of Japan

Tsunamis have been documented striking the islands of Japan more often than anywhere else around the world, so perhaps it is fitting that the word the world uses to describe these waves is Japanese. *Tsunami* is a combination of the words *tsun* (harbor) and *ami* (wave) and is rooted in the Japanese observations of waves of water sweeping through harborside villages and towns, destroying homes, fishing boats, and lives in the process. The ancient Japanese usually attributed tsunamis to divine action and therefore generally accepted them as an unpreventable part of their lives.

Early European observers were less familiar with these waves and their destruction in their part of the world, but they also felt unable to prevent them. They called them "tidal waves," implying that they were merely a result of an abnormally high and destructive tide. But scientists today know that tsunamis are unrelated to tidal action. Instead, these destructive waves are caused by water displacement somewhere on the globe.

Displacement Disturbs Equilibrium

Water displacement occurs when a body of water is disturbed by an object or otherwise caused to move. The inevitable result of such a disturbance is a compensating motion by the water.

This can be easily demonstrated on a small scale with a glass of water and an ice cube. If an ice cube is placed in a full glass of water, the amount of water that spills over the side of the glass is equal to the volume of the ice cube below the waterline. Equilibrium has been restored because an amount of water from the glass equal to the volume of the ice cube below the water's surface has been displaced from the glass.

Nichiren Calming the Storm, *by Utagawa Kuniyoshi. Tsunamis were a popular subject of ancient Japanese art.*

Returning to Equilibrium

Anyone who has played with water has discovered that it is possible to create large waves in many ways. A child sliding back and forth vigorously enough in a bathtub can send bathwater crashing in wave after wave against the sides or out of the tub. Similarly, jumping into a puddle can splash water out of the depression that forms the puddle.

In a sense, both of these activities simulate causes of tsunamis. The water in the bathtub or in the puddle has had something disturb its equilibrium. Once the child in the bathtub stops sliding about, the waves of water slowly grow smaller and smaller and no longer crash against or over the side of the tub. After a foot stomps into a puddle, the water displaced by the invading volume of the boot rushes outward. The water may rebound against the edge of the depression, flowing back and forth with diminishing size and force across the youngster's boot for a few seconds until the water finally comes to rest. The level of the puddle's water has reached equilibrium and has accommodated the intrusion of the boot.

The tsunamis that race across the Pacific Ocean and other bodies of water around the world are very similar. But on a global scale, it takes much longer for tsunami waves to diminish and for waters to return to equilibrium. On a website titled "Questions and Answers on Current Topics in Geosciences," the University of Wollongong's Edward Bryant says, "In some cases, for Pacific Ocean tsunamis, there have been as many as a hundred waves arriving at a coast over a period of 24 hours with diminishing wave heights." Only in the twenty-fifth hour is equilibrum restored.

Sequential photos show the rising waters of a tsunami as it hits the island of Oahu, in Hawaii. An earthquake in Alaska disrupted the equilibrium of water throughout the Pacific Ocean, causing the tsunami that hit Hawaii.

In a similar fashion, tossing a pebble into a pond will generate waves that ripple out from where the pebble hit the water. The small waves radiate out in increasingly larger circles away from the pebble, and eventually the pond surface becomes calm again as the ripples become smaller and farther away from the pebble. Eventually, the waves will become too small to notice; at this point, the water in the pond has compensated for the addition of the pebble by rising to accommodate its volume. Since the pond is much larger than the pebble, the pond's water level is hardly changed. But if a large boulder is tossed into a very small pond, the water level will change dramatically and violently, and water will be pushed out of the pond into the adjacent terrestrial environment.

On a much larger scale, the oceans on earth are, in a sense, one giant pond. Because all the major oceans of the planet are connected, events that occur on one ocean can affect others nearby or thousands of miles away. When water is displaced somewhere around the world, tsunamis may occur. And in the majority of cases, water movements that generate tsunamis are the results of earthquakes, landslides, and volcanic eruptions.

Earthquakes and Tsunamis

Earthquakes that occur underwater or at the edge of the sea are one of the leading causes of tsunamis. Earthquakes that occur on land are familiar events to millions of the world's citizens. But undersea quakes generate less attention, because the movement may not be felt on land. However, if such an earthquake generates a tsunami that strikes a populated shoreline, scientists may study the event for years. To understand how earthquakes can cause tsunamis, one must have an understanding of the major causes of earthquakes.

Earthquakes occur when movement takes place along faults, or areas where rocks of the earth's crust come in contact with one another. Some faults move gradually and their movements are rarely felt. In fact, each year, hundreds of thousands of small tremors register on laboratory instruments but are not felt by humans. Other faults, however, stay motionless, or locked, for many years, building up energy. When the strain on the adjoining rocks finally becomes too much, the fault moves, and the pent-up energy radiates out from the fault as an earthquake.

In general, movement along faults occurs in three ways: thrusting, spreading, and slipping. Thrust faults occur when one portion of the earth's crust is being pushed over the top of another; earthquakes occur when the overriding rocks move up and over the neighboring crust. Spreading, or normal, faults occur when two sections of crust are moving away from each other, triggering wave motion by either pushing the water up or pulling it down. Slipping, or strike-slip, faults occur when one portion of the crust is sliding past another. As Costas Synolakis of the University of Southern California explains, tsunamis are generally associated with thrust faults and with normal faults: "Only those faults that have predominantly vertical displacement and create sufficiently large scale sea-floor deformations or landslides appear to trigger a tsunami."[4]

Regardless of an earthquake's cause, when the tremors cease, there may be other events precipitated by the seismic activity. On land, buildings may have damaged walls and foundations; highway overpasses may crumble; and water and gas pipelines may be bent or ruptured. If the earthquake's motion occurs underwater, however, even though no man-made structures may have been affected, the surrounding rocks may have become fractured and exposed to seawater. This can lead to one of the most dangerous aftereffects of undersea earthquakes: landslides.

Mass Movements of Earth Below the Water

Underwater earthquakes may cause large areas of land to become fractured for miles along a fault line. Under the influence of gravity and the surrounding water, some of these areas will weaken and lose contact with the surrounding rock and crash downward, sometimes for thousands of feet. These landslides, either underwater or at the edge of the seas, push water aside as the mass of rock falls. The displaced water radiates out from the site of the slide, which in turn generates wave actions and, perhaps, tsunamis. Landslides without earthquake triggers also

The San Andreas Fault, shown here, is related to frequent earthquake activity on land. Underwater earthquakes cause water displacement, which in turn can lead to tsunamis.

occur underwater merely as a result of the undersea topography. Landslides consisting of thousands of cubic kilometers of earth do not always generate tsunamis, but they leave their traces in the geologic record. Tsunami researcher Edward Bryant, of Australia's University of Wollongong, reports that "the Agulhas slide off the South African Coast contain[ed] a total of twenty thousand cubic kilometers of material."[5] This landslide occurred in prehistoric times, but a landslide that big today could have devastating effects on populated areas.

In fact, tsunami researchers have turned their focus to underwater landslides and have begun to theorize that some of the world's most devastating tsunamis may have been more directly attributable to landslides than to the earthquakes that precipitated them. Researchers are also focusing their efforts on mapping the areas of the continental shelf off both the east and the west coasts of the United States for areas that might be susceptible to undersea landslides. Since such landslides can generate local tsunamis that could hit a coastal area in as little as five minutes, researchers are becoming increasingly concerned about areas of the ocean floor that had drawn little attention until now.

One area of concern lies off the mid-Atlantic coast. In 1999, researchers Neal Driscoll of the Woods Hole Oceanographic Institute in Massachusetts, Jeffrey Weissel of Columbia University's Lamont-Doherty Earth Observatory, and John Goff of the University of Texas at Austin discovered a twenty-five-mile-long series of roof-shingle-shaped cracked ridges located three hundred to six hundred feet below the ocean surface just north of Cape Hatteras in North Carolina. The cracks, located at the edge of the continental shelf where the ocean floor drops off steeply, could conceivably cause the seabed to crumble, creating an underwater landslide, or slump. The scientists estimated that such a slump would involve a layer of sediment between 100 and 200 meters thick, with a volume of approximately 150 cubic kilometers that would roar down the continental slope, sucking down the seawater behind it. This could generate a tsunami or a series of tsunamis that could reach East Coast cities like Norfolk, Virginia, or Baltimore, Maryland, in as little as twenty minutes. According to Driscoll, public awareness of tsunamis is limited in comparison to knowledge of hurricanes and other coastal storms:

> Tsunamis resulting from offshore earthquakes, landslides and volcanic activity are just as destructive but are not as common. As a result, public awareness is limited, as is our ability to forecast when and where they will strike. . . . Any future submarine landslides starting on this crack system might trigger a tsunami that poses a danger to populations along the nearby coast, and we should know what the risks are for that happening.[6]

For now, the researchers will keep a close eye on the cracks. As Driscoll, Weissel, and Goff write, "It seems wise to invest effort to determine whether [these cracks] are fossil features or are active and likely to produce a potential disastrous, large submarine slide in the near future."[7] If signs of movement are recorded, researchers plan to install special monitoring equipment that they hope will allow them to gauge the extent of the undersea activity before a slump, and any possible tsunamis, occurs.

Researchers are continuing to identify these unanticipated areas that may lead to tsunami activity. These tsunamigenic areas are in contrast to some other areas that are more noticeable, either on land or underwater. For instance, volcanic activity can also create tsunamis.

Volcanic Triple Threat

Volcanic eruptions release lava, gas, and sometimes ash. If the volcano is on land, the lava flows out onto the earth and the gas and ash are released into the atmosphere. Moderate eruptions that have an almost routine, day-to-day nature, such as Hawaii's Kilauea, release lava and gas fairly constantly and cause little anxiety as far as tsunamis are concerned.

Nevertheless, volcanoes are of great concern to tsunami researchers. In particular, those that are underwater or at the water's edge, and especially those that have suddenly begun to stir to life,

The eruption of Mount St. Helens in 1980 caused a massive landslide that buried the surrounding area in 150 feet of earth and rock. Had this eruption taken place underwater, the resulting tsunami would have been enormous.

During an underwater eruption such as this one of the Kavachi volcano near the Solomon Islands, gases rush to the surface, displacing the water and causing tsunamis.

pose three tsunamigenic threats. First, the volcano's sudden eruption could destroy part or all of the volcano's walls, hurtling rocks and ash into the water. The explosion of Mount St. Helens in Washington in 1980, for example, created a landslide that measured 23 square miles, moved up to 150 miles an hour, and buried adjoining areas at an average depth of 150 feet. The amount of water that would have been displaced if this had been an undersea eruption is almost incalculable.

A second threat comes from the pressure of gases released from an underwater volcano. During an eruption, these gases will rush to the surface, displacing tons of water and forcing it to seek equilibrium. A similar effect is observed when a bottle of soda is shaken and then opened quickly. When it is opened, the carbonation, which is from a gas called carbon dioxide, rushes through the small opening at the top, bringing the liquid soda with it. But if the same bottle is opened slowly, the release is much less explosive. By the same token, a volcano in a gradual eruption releases its gases gradually, whereas a violent eruption leads to an explosive release of gases, as well as a more abrupt displacement of water and a greater threat for tsunami formation.

The third threat posed by volcanic eruptions comes from pyroclastic flows. According to Professor Joe Monaghan of Australia's Monash University, volcanoes "emit what are called pyroclastic flows, fast moving hot gas carrying a great deal of solid material that just pushes into the sea and in pushing into the sea it initiates . . . tsunamis."[8] Monaghan, a professor of mathematics, believes that such flows may have been partly responsible for the Thera and Crete tsunamis. He is developing computer models and miniature volcano simulations to try to mimic the interaction between pyroclastic flows and tsunamis. He hopes that this painstaking work will lead to a better understanding of how tsunamis may be generated by this aspect of volcanic activity.

Volcanic activity, along with earthquakes and landslides, cause the vast majority of tsunamis around the world. But geologists have also discovered that, during the earth's history, tsunamis have occurred when water was displaced at the surface by the impact of a large object. Most of these prehistoric waves, or paleotsunamis, are evident only through the record they have left behind in our planet's rocks. These type of tsunamis are rare events, yet scientists are discovering that they have occurred more frequently than previously thought. The only things large enough to hit the world's oceans and cause a tsunami are meteorites or comets.

A Local Catastrophe and a Global Cataclysm

About 65 million years ago, a comet slammed into the earth near the present-day Gulf of Mexico, and, according to Edward Bryant, "a tsunami 100 [meters] high . . . rolled into the southern United States."[9] The comet was about 10 to 15 kilometers in diameter and left a hole 180 kilometers in diameter. The tremendous force of the resulting huge waves tossed together vegetation, sand, clay, and limestone bedrock, as well as pieces of the comet. The waves roared outward from the impact site and across the landscape. Undoubtedly, the force of the tsunamis killed all plants and animals in their path.

Today, rock layers testify to these catastrophic events. The impact crater lies partially on Mexico's Yucatan Peninsula, but the geology as far away as Haiti demonstrates the power of the tsunamis. Geologists have identified a series of rock layers, called a unit, that tells part of the story of the tsunamis' passage. The unit is composed of limestone-rich clay topped by limestone ripped from the bedrock and overlain by at least two meters of sand. Scientists have traced this unit from the Yucatan through Texas and into Alabama, over a distance of more than two thousand kilometers. Other units feature a chaotic mix of vegetation, chunks of the seabed, and sand, suggesting that over the next few days, the region was repetitively swept by tsunamis of diminishing size. Of course, "diminishing size" is a relative description considering that the waves that began the catastrophe were the height of a thirty-story building.

The comet's impact generated more than this local inundation. The two fireballs that followed the crash vaporized the surrounding rock and generated enough heat to burn all the vegetation up to several thousand miles away. Poisonous gases such as carbon dioxide and sulfur dioxide, and perhaps as much as 100 billion tons of dust, choked the atmosphere. The dust traveled around the world, and scientists believe that it shut out so much sunlight that photosynthesis ceased for two to six months. In other words, nothing green could grow.

As the plants died from lack of sunlight, and the food chain that they supported collapsed, entire populations of animals died. The planet suffered a cataclysm that extended far beyond the comet's impact. The tsunamis that followed the impact certainly caused a great deal of destruction to the local ecosystem as well. Many scientists believe that the comet's impact may be the reason that the most populous animals of the day—the dinosaurs—became extinct.

Although there are no other ways to reconstruct this event beyond an examination of the rock record and scientific speculation, other paleotsunamis have been linked to the oral histories of native peoples from the Pacific Northwest to Australia. These witnesses recounted the streaking objects in the sky or the earth's movements, the water's disturbances, and the giant waves that followed. These histories have aided modern scientists in reconstructing some events that are present in the rock record, but oral histories are not always reliable. Some ancient disaster stories have been told so many times that they have acquired the status of legends, with no real scientific value.

Tsunamis in Fact and Fiction

Tsunamis are the subject of many legends and stories, and it is often difficult to separate the fact from fiction. The Atlantis story may be an example of a narrative that grew from a few facts about the tsunamis that devastated Thera and Crete and became a legend immortalized by stories, songs, and films. However, there are a number of myths that exist about tsunamis, and knowing the difference between fact and fiction can save lives.

The popular image of a tsunami as a huge, breaking wave is generally untrue. Katsushika Hokusai, a Japanese artist

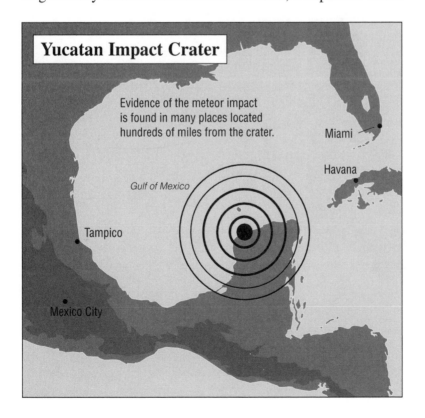

Yucatan Impact Crater

Evidence of the meteor impact is found in many places located hundreds of miles from the crater.

Miami

Havana

Gulf of Mexico

Tampico

Mexico City

who lived in the late eighteenth and early nineteenth centuries, produced a depiction of such a wave dwarfing Mt. Fuji in a series of works called "Thirty-six Views of Fuji." Over the years, many people have represented this wave as a tsunami, but in fact tsunamis rarely have this breaking characteristic. Tsunamis tend to hit land not as a wave that would appeal to surfers but as a solid, vertical mass of water without a breaking crest. According to author Douglas Myles, tsunamis can "take the form of a sudden and very rapid rising of the tide, with the inrushing water cresting far above the normal high tide mark, presenting a very turbulent front which nonetheless fails to break at the peak of its force but instead dissolves into foam at some distance inland." [10]

Because these walls of water have little or no break to the crest, observers on shore may be unaware of their presence or approach, and thus have no way to estimate their speed. Observers who venture to the shore to observe a tsunami do not realize its

Under the Wave off Kanagawa, *part of Katsushika Hokusai's "Thirty-six Views of Fuji," depicts an enormous wave towering over Mt. Fuji.*

power and are often under the mistaken impression that they can outrun the water if it comes too close. Some survive to tell of their narrow escape from the onrushing waters; many do not.

With Unexpected Speed

Many people who underestimate how fast tsunamis travel often end up becoming unwitting witnesses (or even victims) to the waves' power, for another enduring misconception about tsunamis is their rate of speed when approaching and eventually hitting coastal areas. Perhaps this misconception is due to the lingering use of the inaccurate term *tidal wave.*

Coastal residents who are aware that their area may be hit by a tsunami sometimes wrongly expect the event to occur as an abnormally high incoming tide. In most places on earth, high tides arrive and rise gently and almost imperceptibly. Tsunamis, on the other hand, arrive with unexpected sound and fury. According to Eddie Bernard of the National Oceanographic and Atmospheric Administration (NOAA), the tsunami "makes a very loud sound as it comes barreling [in] from the ocean into the coast line at about twenty-five to thirty miles per hour,"[11] making it impossible for humans to outrun it without a head start. In addition, observers who somehow manage to get out of the way of the incoming wave may be under the impression that the worst is over. That is rarely the case.

The Next Wave . . . and the Next

Tsunami waves are not tidal phenomena. Thus, unlike tides, another tsunami may be just a few minutes behind the first terrifying wall of water.

Like a pebble tossed in a pond, a tsunami generates waves rippling out from its initial point of impact. This collection of waves is called a wave train. Tsunamis move in a wave train. Bernard says that, after the first wave recedes, "another wave will approach some ten to twenty minutes later, and this process will be repeated about three [times], so the entire episode will last over an hour, with a series of three to maybe four or even five waves."[12] In addition, the second and third waves in the train may be higher and more powerful than the first. Their destructive power comes not only from their sheer size and volume but from the debris left behind after the first wave hits. The splintered docks and piers, the shattered walls of buildings, and the damaged and displaced metal objects as large as trucks and ships resulting from the first wave can be added to the next wave's waters as they rush inland. The misconception that the

Hilo, Hawaii, April 1, 1946

Hawaii was hit by a tsunami on April Fool's Day 1946 after an earthquake off Alaska's Aleutian Islands generated a series of waves that raced across the Pacific Ocean. Walter C. Dudley and Min Lee, in their book *Tsunami!* recount the experience of a young man who was on his way to school when the waves hit the town of Hilo.

On the early school bus that carried Bunji Fujimoto to school that morning, . . . laughter of disbelief greeted the information volunteered by some, as the bus came down the hill, that the sea had receded and left the ocean floor bare. When the doubters were finally persuaded to look from the bus window, however, they discovered it was not a joke. Excited by this unusual event, but completely unaware of its significance, some left the bus as soon as it stopped and ran to the seawall. Others, a little more cautious, or less curious, stayed on the grass. Bunji was one of those who kept his distance from the ocean. As he watched his more daring classmates and his brother, he saw the water rise over the seawall. At first he did not realize the danger. It was not a crashing, breaking wave, but an ever-rising, ever-encroaching wall of water that flowed without stopping. Scared now, he turned and ran across the grass toward the higher ground. Other students fled behind him, and he noticed a member of the basketball team who made good use of his long legs, for he had been on the ocean side of the seawall when the wave began to surge; with his natural speed enhanced by terror, he achieved safety. Some were overwhelmed by the wave but not dragged out to sea because they became stuck in the bushes. Others, like Bunji's younger brother, were swallowed by the onrushing sea and never seen again.

A tsunami destroys a pier at the town of Hilo, Hawaii.

worst is over once the initial wave has struck has led people to return to the coastline to survey the damage, and many of these individuals become victims to the next waves.

Staying Aware and Alert

The key to separating fact from fiction about tsunamis and other natural phenomena lies in education and training. Coastal residents need to be aware of the potential hazards that exist in their areas, and need to be alert to changing conditions both above ground and underwater. Both professional and amateur scientists can easily take note of earthquake and volcanic activity that occurs above ground, but they should not overlook undersea activity as well. Such potential areas of activity need to be recorded and monitored for changes to ensure that an earthquake, landslide, or volcanic eruption that triggers the next tsunami finds coastal populations mindful of its cause, aware of the danger, and prepared for its consequences.

A Growing Wave

To understand the forces responsible for the formation of tsunamis, one must first understand the basic forces at work within the earth. These forces are an integral part of the ever-changing planet on which we live, and have built the earth's mountains and shaped continents and oceans. They continue to fascinate amateur and professional observers alike, and are responsible for earthquakes, landslides, volcanoes, and tsunamis.

The study of tsunamis involves several areas, including geology, physics, and mathematics. Geologists who study tsunamis may specialize in seismology (the study of earth movements) or in volcanology (the study of volcanoes). Physicists may specialize in fluid mechanics (the study of how water and gases move) or in geophysics (how earth movements are related to friction, gravity, and sound waves). Mathematicians contribute to the study of tsunamis by developing models of wave movement, height, speed, and potential damage.

Each of these specialized fields has contributed to our understanding of the earth's behavior. Each helps other researchers observe conditions around the world in anticipation of potential tsunamis. And each helps us to understand both the tsunamigenic actions at work and the conditions that exist before a tsunami is formed.

Waiting and Listening

Just as earth scientists have discovered that certain activities lead to conditions that create tsunamis, they have also learned that tsunamis occur with greatest frequency in certain areas of the planet. Scientists have identified these areas with the assistance of plate tectonics, which is the study of the interaction of the earth's various crustal plates. Knowledge gained from plate tectonics has enabled researchers to concentrate on the most active areas in anticipation of future tsunamis and to formulate theories about what may have contributed to historic tsunamis.

Since tsunami researchers have discovered that the majority of tsunamis are generated by earthquakes and earthquake-related activities (including some landslides), they wait for and listen to

Plate Tectonics

The understanding of the earth's dynamic behavior has changed dramatically in the last fifty years thanks to the theory of plate tectonics. Earth and marine scientist Ellen Prager, in her book *Furious Earth: The Science and Nature of Earthquakes, Volcanoes, and Tsunamis,* describes the range of the discipline:

> Few other scientific revelations can surpass plate tectonics in helping understand the present, past and future shape of the Earth's surface, and its earth-shaking, fiery, and watery displays of power.

> Before plate tectonics and studies in modern earth science, people generally thought that the planet was solid throughout its interior and fixed on the surface. But the Earth is now known to be a dynamic sphere whose hot interior moves in slow motion and whose surface shifts and changes with time. The planet's hard surface is relatively thin and composed of a series of interlocking, rigid pieces or plates that move atop a layer of hotter, more fluidlike material—akin to a Milky Way candy bar with a hard, thin layer of brittle chocolate overlying a softer, more fluid caramel layer below. The Earth's internal layering plays a fundamental role in plate tectonics and the planet's furious nature.

> Thus, plates may be spreading away from each other on one part of the globe; they may be moving and grinding past one another; or a heavier, older plate may be forced beneath another, younger and lighter plate. The motion of these plates has helped explain a tremendous amount of geologic evidence and has changed global geologic thinking.

these seismic events around the world. Geologists measure earthquake activity using instruments called seismographs and seismometers. Seismographs record the arrival of various types of shock waves that pass through the earth's layers, and their readings help researchers determine the location and relative size of the quake. Seismometers record the movement of the earth directly, and are usually placed along fault zones where historic activity has occurred. The information from these instruments allows seismologists to rate each earthquake's magnitude on the Richter scale, which offers a way of describing the amount of energy released by a quake.

Although there are hundreds of thousands of earthquakes around the world every year, few are powerful enough to register significantly on the Richter scale. According to Edward Bryant, "only 10% of these occur under an ocean with movement that is favourable for the generation of tsunami[s]. Earthquake-generated tsunami[s] are associated with seismic events registering more than 6.5 on the Richter scale."[13]

Seismologic networks around the world are maintained by government agencies, such as the United States Geologic Survey (USGS), and by universities that specialize in earthquake studies, such as the University of California at Berkeley. They pool their information with other networks in order to pinpoint an earthquake's size and location, known as its epicenter. Other organizations, such as the National Weather Service's U.S. West Coast and Alaska Tsunami Warning Center (WC/ATWC) in Palmer, Alaska, have established seismologic networks purely for the purpose of identifying potentially tsunamigenic earthquakes. Any time the network's instruments record a seismic event, warning alarms go off inside the center to alert the staff of the tremors. The WC/ATWC's original mission included "the issuing of tsunami warnings to California, Oregon, Washington, and British Columbia, for potential tsunamigenic earthquakes occurring in their coastal areas," but in 1996, its responsibility was expanded "to include all Pacific-wide tsunamigenic sources which could affect the California, Oregon, Washington, British Columbia and Alaska coasts."[14]

Networks similar to the WC/ATWC also exist in other nations that surround the Pacific Ocean basin. This is the world's most

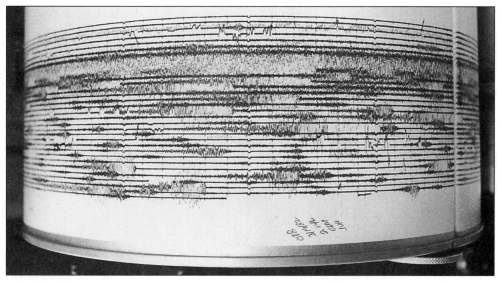

A seismograph records shock waves that pass through the earth. Scientists use instruments like this to determine the location and size of earthquakes.

active area for earthquakes, volcanoes, and tsunamis because of the interactions between several different plates. Geologists call this area the "Ring of Fire."

The Ring of Fire

There are several tectonic events occurring in the region of the Pacific Ocean. The Pacific Plate is moving past the North American Plate along California's famous San Andreas Fault. At the same time, the Pacific Plate is also being overridden, or subducted, by the North American, Eurasian, Australian, and Philippine Plates, creating areas of earthquakes as well as volcanoes from the Gulf of Alaska in the northeast, to the east coast of Russia and to Japan in the northwest, to the Marianas Island chain in the west, and to the Indonesia, New Guinea, and New Zealand island areas in the west and south. Furthermore, off the coast of South America, the Nazca Plate is moving away from the Pacific Plate along the East Pacific Rise and is being overridden by the South American Plate.

When one plate is forced beneath another along a subduction zone, the plates form a feature that geologists call a trench. The trenches around the Pacific basin have been the source of most of the tsunamigenic earthquakes in recent history. For example, the impetus for the establishment of the West Coast and Alaska Tsunami Warning Center was several tsunamis that hit Alaska in 1964. The tsunamis were generated by an earthquake measuring 8.5 on the Richter scale and the subsequent landslides that were related to movement along the Aleutian Trench. And the Java Trench, where the Australian plate dives beneath the Eurasian plate, was responsible for one of the most famous volcanic eruptions and associated tsunamis in history, which took place at Krakatau in Indonesia in 1883.

Krakatau, August 27, 1883

In 1883, the modern nation of Indonesia was a Dutch colony where rubber, timber, coffee, rice, and other natural resources were being developed and harvested. In the Sunda Strait, between

the large islands of Sumatra and Java, a small collection of volcanic islands was beginning to stir to life. Volcanic islands in that part of the world are not unusual, and earthquakes and eruptions are an accepted part of life. The largest of these islands, called by the natives Krakatau (but sometimes misspelled "Krakatoa"), was showing signs of erupting, but few observers could have imagined what would happen when Krakatau erupted in August.

Several small eruptions were followed by three eruptions on August 27 that virtually destroyed the island. According to Edward Bryant,

> [The] third blast was the largest sound ever heard by humanity and was recorded 4,800 km [kilometers] away on the island of Rodriguez in the Indian Ocean. . . . Windows 150 km away were shattered. The atmospheric shock wave traveled around the world seven times. Barometers in Europe and the United States measured significant oscillations in pressure over nine days following the blast. The total energy released by the third eruption was equivalent to 200 megatons of [the explosive] TNT. [15]

The atmospheric shock wave from this eruption produced tsunamis that not only were greater than others ever recorded but were measured almost around the world. The explosive change in atmospheric pressure destroyed the equilibrium of the surrounding waters and drove them away from Krakatau in massive surges; more than thirty-six hours later, tsunami waves were still being recorded across the Pacific Ocean and as far away as the English Channel.

Although scientists agree that the cause of the tsunamis that followed the third eruption was the massive, almost instantaneous change in atmospheric pressure, they debate what caused the tsunamis that were generated by the first two eruptions. Seismologists, geophysicists, and mathematicians have modeled these first two eruptions and theorize that the tsunamis that followed could have been formed under four different circumstances, based on eyewitness accounts and subsequent investigations: pyroclastic flows from the volcano, a lateral blast as the volcano erupted through its side, the collapse of the caldera, and a submarine, or underwater, explosion. Each event accounts for only part of the tsunami record, so it remains for future investigators to try to piece together exactly what happened at Krakatau.

Piecing together the events associated with a historic tsunami can be like detective work. The scientists need to gather evidence, examine the clues, and suggest theories as to what happened. As the causes of tsunamis become better known through geophysical and seismological research, the behavior of tsunamis becomes an increasingly important area of research. Physicists who specialize in fluid mechanics study how these waves form, how they behave differently from wind-generated waves, and how they behave when they strike land.

The Nature of Waves

Any investigation of tsunami behavior requires a familiarity with several general aspects of waves. Certain terms are used consistently. The top of any wave is called a crest; the bottom of a wave is called a trough. The distance between any two crests or between two troughs is called the wavelength. The height between the crest and the trough is called the wave's amplitude. The time it takes for a crest and a trough to pass a given area is called the wave's period. Both tsunamis and wind-generated waves have crests, troughs, wavelength, amplitude, and periods, but Daniel Pendick of New York City's WNET notes that "calling [tsunamis] by the same name as the ordinary wind-driven [wave] variety is a bit like referring to firecrackers and atomic warheads both as 'explosives.' . . . [A] tsunami represents a vast volume of seawater in motion—the source of its destructive power." [16]

The power behind a tsunami is partly a function of the amount of seawater in motion. Wind-generated waves can take on great heights when stirred up by strong winds, but an amplitude exceeding one hundred feet or so is rare in the open ocean. Such waves are actually disturbing only the top of the ocean; several feet beneath the surface, the water is generally unaffected by the turbulence above.

Tsunamis, however, are a different matter. A tsunami water column on the move contains thousands of times more water than a surface wave, but the disturbance of surface water at the onset is almost undetectable. Wind-generated waves will have a wavelength of less than a foot to over five hundred feet, and periods of approximately 0.2 seconds to 30 seconds. Tsunamis, on the other hand, typically have wavelengths hundreds of miles long and periods lasting from ten minutes to more than an hour. Costas Synolakis says,

> Wind waves vary in height from tiny ripples on the sea surface to rogue waves 30 m [meters] tall. Tsunamis, on the other hand, race across the open ocean as a series of long, low-crested waves, usually less than 1 to 2 m (1 to 6 ft) high. In fact, until they reach the coast, these mountains of water are benign beasts, virtually imperceptible to the human eye. A ship out at sea may sit completely unaware as a deadly tsunami passes beneath the hull. [17]

Volcanic eruptions at the island of Krakatau in 1883 caused the largest tsunamis ever recorded. The large island was split into two, and tsunamis were recorded as far away as the English Channel.

The amount of energy within a tsunami far exceeds that of even the tallest wind-driven wave. Alastair Sarre of the Australian Academy of Science points out that the energy in a wave "is proportional to the length (the distance between two crests of the wave) and to the square of the height (the distance between the trough and the crest)."[18] This means that the energy of a tsunami in the deep ocean, which may have a height of less than three feet but a wavelength of up to five hundred miles, is spread out across the ocean. It also means that a tsunami in the open ocean will maintain most of its energy as long as it is traveling through deep water.

The challenge facing tsunami researchers is not just in calculating the amount of water that has been affected by a seismic or volcanic event but also in calculating a potential tsunami's speed and direction. Moreover, because deformations in the seafloor due to earthquakes, landslides, volcanoes, or extraterrestrial im-

An earthquake-generated tsunami floods a coastal area. Tsunamis in deep water are not tall but have wavelengths of many miles. When tsunamis approach land, the wavelength gets smaller, pushing the waves to great heights.

pact will affect the height of the water column, the research requires an understanding of the seafloor topography where the column is disturbed as well as the topography in a potential tsunami's path. Specialists in fluid mechanics and mathematics work to correlate the many changing variables with the aim of creating accurate large-scale and fine-scale models to help scientists learn more about these great waves.

Investigating Tsunamis by Means of Modeling

At first glance, calculating a tsunami's potential speed along a stretch of seafloor is a matter of simple algebra. The wave's velocity can be calculated by taking the square root of the product of the depth of the water multiplied by the speed of gravity, which is a constant 32 feet per second squared. So, for example, if part of the seafloor of the Pacific Ocean undergoes deformation at its average depth of 3.5 miles (or 18,480 feet), the velocity of a tsunami generated there would be the square root of the product of 18,480 times 32 feet per second squared, which reduces to the square root of 591,360 feet per second. This square root equals approximately 769 feet per second, or 524 miles per hour.

If the seafloor had the same depth everywhere, tsunami velocity calculations would be easy. However, the ocean floors around the world are dotted with ridges, canyons, plateaus, and underwater mountains, all of which can affect the speed of a tsunami. So, when estimating the speed of a newly formed series of waves, tsunami specialists generally use an average for the depth of the ocean that the tsunami will cross. This will give researchers a "best guess" for the waves' velocity.

Scientists who try to model the behavior of coastal and wind-driven waves generally use wave tanks. Wave tanks, also called directional wave basins, look like swimming pools but have several features that help researchers study wave behavior. A piston-driven wave generator, a wall at one end of the tank, pushes water at a controlled rate to create experiments to study wave action. The tank may also have glass walls to facilitate underwater scientific observations. Because such tanks have a given depth and volume of water, they have proven valuable in studying open-ocean wave behavior. Tsunami researchers have discovered that

Krakatau, August 27, 1883

On August 27, 1883, N.H. van Sandick, a public works engineer for the Dutch government, was on board a coastal steamer called the *Governor General Loudon* as it lay in the harbor of the port of Telok Betong, on the island of Sumatra, in modern-day Indonesia. His observations of the tsunamis following the Krakatau eruptions are found in *Krakatau 1883: The Volcanic Eruption and Its Effects* by Tom Simkin and Richard S. Fiske:

> Suddenly, at about 7 A.M., a tremendous wave came moving in from the sea, which literally blocked the view and moved with tremendous speed. . . . The ship made a tremendous tumbling; however, the wave had passed and the *Loudon* was saved. The wave now reached Telok Betong and raced inland. Three more similar colossal waves followed, which destroyed all of Telok Betong right before our eyes.

> [Later that day, the] sea became stormy. The wind increased and became a flying hurricane. Following, there were a series of sea tremors. These evidenced themselves by very high waves, which formed suddenly. A few of these hit the *Loudon* sideways, so that she was lifted up and leaned sideways to the extent that danger of capsizing threatened. The ship then made motions, so that everything rolled over. . . .

> These were hours which were not lightly forgotten. After each sea tremor, an amazing stillness and calmness of the sea existed, and also the muddy rain [of volcanic ash] stopped temporarily. This calm was even more disquieting than the hurricane.

wave tanks currently in use can yield valuable information about tsunami formation and behavior as well, but appropriately scaled-up basins could assist modeling experiments even further.

Tsunamis in Miniature

The greatest challenge in simulating tsunamis in a wave tank is dealing with the scale of these great waves. Since wind-driven waves affect only the top layer of water, they can be reproduced quite accurately. Reproducing tsunamis, however, proves more difficult. A scientist who wishes to model a 1-meter high tsunami on an ocean 2,000 meters deep, for example, might attempt to use a scale of 1:100. A tank 20 meters (65 feet) deep would fit the 1:100 scale, but this would mean that any resulting wave would be a mere one centimeter, or less than half an inch, in height. Complicating matters even further are the exceedingly long wavelengths of tsunamis. As Costas Synolakis says, "A typical tsunami in the open ocean might have a wavelength of 100 kilometers; using 1:100 scaling, the model wave would have to be one kilometer long!"[19] A tank of water big enough to model a tsunami realistically would have to be an unthinkable twenty meters deep by one thousand meters long. (By comparison, an Olympic-sized swimming pool is generally no more than five meters deep and only fifty meters long.) And to model a tsunami approaching the shore from three hundred kilometers away, researchers would need a tank that was even larger.

For all these reasons, fluid mechanics specialists and mathematicians are increasingly teaming up to develop computer-generated simulations of tsunami behavior. At Monash University, math professor Joe Monaghan has worked with geologist Ray Cas and other researchers from the Department of Earth Sciences to study these fluid movements at sea and as they approach and hit land. According to Tim Thwaites, in the university's *Monash Magazine,*

> The upshot of the research has been the coming together at Monash of a multidisciplinary group of researchers interested in modeling the key features of large-scale earth movements, volcanoes, earthquakes, landslides, tsunamis and the like. They now work in a new laboratory known as Epsilon—the Earth Process Simulation Laboratory—which has been fitted out with wave tanks and several high-speed computers.[20]

Other research centers are developing similar specialized facilities or are striving to upgrade their current capabilities. For example, Oregon State University recently received a grant from the National Science Foundation to expand its directional wave basin from the present dimensions of 26.5 meters long, 18.3 meters wide, and 1.52 meters deep to 48.8 meters long, 26.5 meters wide, and 2.0 meters deep. In addition, new computerized equipment will be developed and installed. According to the National Science Foundation's award notice, the equipment will "provide new earthquake engineering research testing capabilities for test and validation of advanced analytical and numerical models of tsunami-wave/structure interactions for a full range of ocean, coastal, and harbor studies."[21] To enhance the study of their simulations, researchers will use digital cameras that will give "multiple, simultaneous frames of reference and fields of view for both local and remote investigators."[22] Furthermore, the university intends to integrate this new equipment into its research program, college-level instruction, and outreach efforts to local schools and communities.

The enhanced wave basin will also provide training opportunities for outside researchers, and Oregon State's Web-based materials will assist university faculty at other institutions in incorporating tsunami test experiences into their courses. The university intends to make all of the data from studies at the tsunami basin available to researchers on the Internet, which no doubt will further increase scientists' understanding of tsunamis.

No matter how much information is gathered by models and computer simulations, tsunami specialists still rely on hard, physical evidence of tsunamis in order to make their laboratory experiments as realistic as possible. Their challenge is to combine real-life information from places hit by tsunamis with their laboratory studies to increase awareness of potentially tsunami-genic conditions and ensure that the word gets out if a tsunami is likely to strike.

Getting the Word Out

In a world that is increasingly connected by communications networks, it is easier than ever for officials to warn coastal populations of possible tsunamis in their areas. Emergency organizations use telephones, radio broadcasts, warning sirens, television bulletins, and the Internet to get the word out as soon as possible so that people have as much time as possible to prepare for the tsunami.

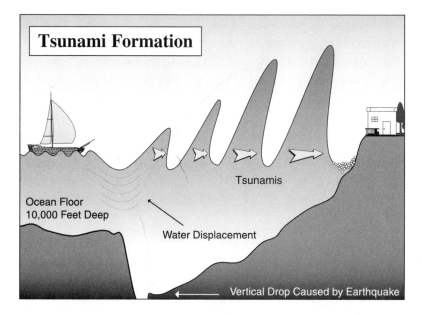

Tsunami Formation

Tsunamis

Ocean Floor
10,000 Feet Deep

Water Displacement

Vertical Drop Caused by Earthquake

In the United States, Canada, and Japan, these warnings may come from a national government agency, a cooperative of research universities, or perhaps a local government. For example, if scientists believed that a tsunami was going to strike the area of Seattle, Washington, warnings would go out from the West Coast and Alaska Tsunami Warning Center in Palmer, Alaska; from NOAA's Pacific Marine Environmental Laboratory (PMEL) in Seattle; and from the University of Washington's Department of Earth and Space Sciences. Each of these agencies makes the information available to the general public through its Internet site. In addition, the U.S. Coast Guard broadcasts tsunami information over marine radio channels for mariners and coastal residents.

Tsunami information for Seattle residents also comes from the local government of King County, Washington. Seattle itself is not directly exposed to the ocean; the Olympic Peninsula and Puget Sound islands shield it from the Pacific. However, earthquakes along the Seattle Fault in the nearby Cascade Mountains could generate tsunamis within Puget Sound, which would give little time for warning and preparation. According to the King County Office of Emergency Management,

For tsunamis generated by local events, . . . the time from initiation of a tsunami to its arrival at shore can be as little as a couple of minutes. Residents in areas susceptible to tsunamis should be made aware of the need to seek high ground if they feel strong ground shaking. Coastal communities should identify evacuation routes even if they do not have good information about potential inundation areas. [23]

Unfortunately, plans for getting the word out to isolated communities and even some entire countries are not as thorough as the system in Seattle. The United Nations is working to improve this situation.

Communication Is the Key

Many nations in the Pacific basin do not have an advanced level of communications that allows widespread emergency information broadcasts. To help improve tsunami alerts, the United Nations Educational, Scientific, and Cultural Organization (UNESCO)'s Intergovernmental Oceanographic Commission (IOC) established an international tsunami warning system called ITSU in 1965 that today tracks sea levels at more than one hundred monitoring stations around the Pacific.

Ideally, coastal communities around the Pacific are notified in advance of the potential for a tsunami in their area. For example, Japan's Meteorological Agency, which monitors seismic activity in the western Pacific Ocean, issued precautionary tsunami warnings for Japan after an earthquake registering 7.1 on the Richter scale occurred on March 31, 2002, off the island of Taiwan. While the quake caused considerable damage on Taiwan, the tsunami warnings were later cancelled. According to a Meteorological Agency official, "We cancelled the warnings because we judged that there was no concern of damage from tsunamis," [24] adding that a tsunami twenty centimeters (eight inches) high was detected at Japan's southern Yonaguni Island and a smaller tsunami occurred at Ishigaki Island before the warnings were cancelled.

For the areas of the world that remain isolated from outside communications networks, however, the prospect of having to mount a rapid response to a tsunami threat is daunting. For example, the Republic of the Philippines, which is located south of Taiwan, might have been affected by postquake tsunamis following the March 31 earthquake. It is unlikely, however, that all the nation's islands would have gotten information about potential tsunamis in time for adequate preparation. Fortunately, the tsunami threat from the recent event turned out to be slight.

Time Is Critical

The key to preparing for tsunamis when the waves start to form is having adequate time. Adequate time is also needed to educate coastal communities about tsunami dangers, to prepare emergency tsunami plans and practice their implementation, and to get out the word that conditions exist that may cause tsunamis. Scientists and community leaders work to develop better cooperative efforts in these areas, but they are constrained by budgeting and commitment priorities. For example, programs to instruct

A meteorologist studies weather patterns to look for any activity that could cause a tsunami. Meteorological agencies around the world are trying to improve the dissemination of tsunami warnings.

citizens with little formal education about the hazards of tsunamis take time to design and take money and governmental commitment to implement.

But even in this age of advanced technology, and along coastlines with tsunami-aware populations, tsunamis have been known to strike with little or no warning. As researchers identify and monitor potential areas for seismic, volcanic, and landslide activity, the public needs to understand the threats these areas may hold, and to take action if somewhere water is displaced, starts to seek equilibrium, and begins to form a tsunami.

A Wall of Water

As a forming tsunami races across an open ocean, there are few ways to record its passage. Its waves are unnoticed by an ocean vessel among the normal swells of the sea. Its transit is unrecorded by weather satellites that can track the development of even the smallest tropical storm. Its speed allows it to strike a coastline with little or no warning. Tsunamis are such rare phenomena that they are seldom observed directly by scientists. Yet those who do observe the tsunamis—the eyewitnesses who survive the rampaging waters—can provide valuable insight into the wave train's behavior and legacy of destruction.

In a world that is increasingly interconnected, the destruction wrought by tsunamis is becoming better understood with each passing event. Historically, the English-speaking populations of the world have rarely been affected by tsunamis, which may explain the inaccessibility of much of the literature on the subject. But in the last fifty years, scientific and emergency response communities around the world have developed new lines of communication and have fostered international partnerships, and these allow a much broader segment of the world's citizens to try to understand the phenomenon of tsunamis. These partnerships and communications networks were in part responsible for the broad-based international attention that was focused on the island nation of Papua New Guinea in 1998.

Papua New Guinea, July 17, 1998

July 17, 1998, was the beginning of a four-day holiday for the nation of Papua New Guinea. On the country's northeastern

Villagers in Papua New Guinea survey debris left by tsunamis in July 1998. The church pictured at right remained intact, but was pushed several hundred feet from its foundation.

coast were the fishing villages of Warupu, Arop, and Malol, located on a sandy strip of land that separates Sissano Lagoon from the Bismarck Sea. As evening fell and the villagers gathered to begin the holiday celebrations, a loud bang "that reportedly sounded much like a jet engine"[25] reverberated through the air. The earthquake that followed did not strike the local people as noteworthy, since tremors are fairly common to the region, and this one did not seem particularly threatening. But shortly after the loud bang, the sea level began to fall, and then a towering wall of water rushed ashore. Survivors of that night's tsunamis—which included three waves in all—told tales of the horizon "getting higher and higher" as a "frothing and sparkling wave"[26] headed toward them, picking up everything in its path and rolling across the narrow ribbon of sand into the lagoon. It was all over in half an hour. But in that time, over 2,000 people died, 1,000 were injured, and 10,000 were left homeless along a twenty-five-kilometer stretch of coastline.

Those who were still alive endured a prolonged nightmare among the cries of the wounded and the bodies of the dead, for the survivors had no way to broadcast their plight. According to Costas Synolakis, "Twelve hours went by before the disaster was even discovered by the outside world, when a helicopter carrying people to a nearby lumber mill flew over the area."[27] Only then did help begin to arrive, and news of the tsunamis reached the scientific community. As researchers began to collect evidence from on-site inspections, interviews with survivors, and seismic data, they began to piece together the events surrounding the Papua New Guinea tsunamis. One observation that many survivors made was that the sea had retreated offshore farther than anyone could remember.

The Waters Recede

The villagers of Papua New Guinea observed a common aspect of tsunamis. Later analysis revealed that the waters receded from the shore because of a hydrodynamic feature that tsunami specialists call a depression wave. A depression wave forms when there is a drop in the overriding water column due to a sudden downward shift of the seabed floor. This change starts the water in motion, and the leading edge of a tsunami may soon form. Philip Watts, of the California Institute of Technology's Engineering and Applied Science Division, says that this gives coastal residents "a bit of warning. If you see the sea receding, get out and stay out!"[28] Unfortunately for those who have never experienced a tsunami, this backward flow may just seem like an abnormally low tide.

Coastal residents are used to the daily movements of the tides. Low tides and high tides are part of the daily rhythm of the waters, and any unexpected change is bound to attract notice. As a tsunami's depression wave approaches and seawater recedes, local residents tend to notice the difference almost immediately. In fact, there are tales of some residents of fishing villages who flocked to the shore to catch the fish that were stranded by the retreating seas. Unfortunately, these individuals soon discovered that they were far too close to an approaching tsunami to reach safety.

The First Tsunami Hits

Tsunamis can remain fairly constant in size and shape in the open ocean, but as they approach land, their character changes. As the first of a series of tsunamis approaches shore, its water column, perhaps thousands of feet in height, begins to encounter more shallow water. Eric Geist of the U.S. Geological Survey—Western Region Coastal and Marine Geology Laboratory explains that several things happen as the waves travel up onto the continental slope: "Most obvious is that the amplitude increases. In addition, the wavelength decreases. This results in steepening of the leading wave,"[29] which is an important factor in the height of the tsunami when it hits land. According to Douglas L. Smith of Caltech,

> A tsunami's height and arrival time are profoundly influenced by the water's depth. As the bottom shoals [reaches a shallow part], the water piles up and the wave slows down. . . . The depth at which the bottom begins steering the wave depends on its wavelength, so for wind-driven waves a few meters apart, only the shallows counts. Tsunamis, however, have wavelengths tens to hundreds of kilometers, so it's *all* shallow water to them—the midocean abyssal plains average about four kilometers deep.[30]

Tsunami velocity and wavelength help determine a wave's destructive potential. Science writer Alastair Sarre elaborates: "As the depth of the water decreases so too do wave length and wave velocity, but the energy invested in the [tsunami] remains nearly constant. . . . [In addition,] wave height increases as the seabed becomes shallower."[31] All waves act in this manner when they approach the shore, but because tsunami waves contain far more energy than wind-driven waves, they will grow significantly greater in height.

The nature of the seabed immediately offshore is also an important factor in how the tsunami behaves when it hits land. After tsunamis struck Nicaragua in 1992 and East Java, Indonesia, in 1994, scientists were eager to learn why these events had been so unexpectedly devastating. Branching out in a new research direction, they began to study the offshore bathymetry, that is, the

A photograph taken a few days after the Papua New Guinea tsunamis shows the location where a village once stood. Three major tsunamis, including one that was twenty-three feet tall, destroyed three villages and killed thousands of people.

shape of the seabed close to shore. They discovered that their thinking and modeling needed to be changed.

The Riddle of Offshore Bathymetry

For scientists, bathymetry covers the entire scope of seabed landforms. Bathymetric studies cover not only deep-sea features such as canyons, trenches, and seamounts but also elements closer to shore such as reefs and sandbars. Studies of the deformation of the deep-sea bathymetric landscape have long been considered the most important aspect in understanding tsunami behavior. Because tsunamis have exponentially more energy than wind-driven waves, which are easily affected by the shape of the seabed floor near the shoreline, scientists believed that offshore bathymetry had little influence on tsunami behavior. However, that belief has changed in recent years. Costas Synolakis states,

One of the puzzling aspects of the damage in the 1992 Nicaraguan tsunami was that along the shore the intensity of the destruction was highly irregular. In some regions little damage was done—even the beach umbrellas were left standing—whereas other sections of the shoreline were completely decimated. In 1995, scientists from USC [University of Southern California], the U.S. Army Coastal Engineering Research Center, and the University of Washington went back to Nicaragua to carefully measure the offshore bathymetry. . . . The survey revealed that at about 200 to 600 meters offshore, most of the Nicaraguan coast is fronted by a submarine coral reef, and the openings in the reef coincided with the greatest amount of tsunami damage.[32]

Water enthusiasts such as surfers and bodyboarders have long known that offshore features like reefs affect how wind-driven waves break along the shore. But now scientists are beginning to recognize that such features seem to also affect the more powerful tsunamis. The nature of the offshore bathymetry helped explain the behavior of the Nicaraguan events, and understanding similar bathymetry at other sites of tsunamis has helped further scientific understanding. Measurements following the Papua New Guinea tsunamis revealed previously unknown faults, ridges, and slump zones in the offshore bathymetry near Sissano Lagoon. Scientists theorize that movements of these localized features might have contributed to the tsunamis' severity in that region since these features were not present where the waves were less devastating, such as just ten kilometers to the west. Despite the valve in such findings, this type of information is usually collected after a tsunami has struck, and while it may go a long way in explaining why a tsunami behaved as it did, it is likely to be of little comfort to those who actually witnessed the destruction.

A Legacy of Destruction

When a tsunami hits, almost everything it encounters is swept along with it. During the tsunamis that followed the eruption of Krakatau, a coastal steamer called the *Berouw* was carried two miles inland and around a bend in a river, where it was gently

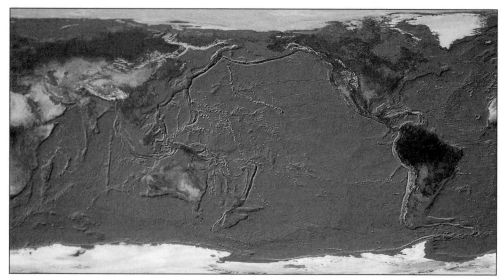

An image of the earth, centered on the Pacific Ocean, shows scientists the position of ridges and faults that can affect the behavior of tsunamis.

set down, upright and almost intact, in a coconut tree grove. In 1964, when several tsunamis slammed into Alaska's southern coast, sailors unloading cargo at the end of a three-hundred-foot pier at Valdez felt the earthquake shake the ten-thousand-ton freighter *Chena* like a rag doll. Then the town disappeared from their view as a tsunami rose higher and higher, soon crushing the port's onshore oil storage facilities, which caught fire as metal ground against metal.

The tsunami that struck Hilo, Hawaii, on April Fool's Day 1946 was generated by an earthquake in Alaska just after midnight on April 1. Tsunamis also struck closer to the source of the quake; the Scotch Cap lighthouse on Unimak Island, Alaska, five stories tall and forty feet above the water, was a mere ninety miles from the epicenter, and was destroyed by a wave at least one hundred feet high. The five Coast Guardsmen inside were killed. The Coast Guard radar station that sat over one hundred feet above the surf and back from the rocky headland was damaged, but the crew survived by reaching higher ground. The same quake sent tsunamis speeding south. They roared ashore at Hilo, Hawaii, less than five hours later, destroying the town's waterfront.

Millions of gallons of water slamming into a coastline have a feared destructive potential. What makes tsunamis even more fascinating is that, once the water hits land, it has to go *somewhere;* it does not just dissipate into spray, as large, breaking, wind-driven waves do. Because tsunami waves generally do not break atop their crests but, instead, move as solid masses, they inundate the immediate coastal area and keep moving inland. The greatest vertical height a tsunami reaches above sea level as it comes onshore is called run-up, and the greatest distance it reaches from shore is called the horizontal inundation distance. Each tsunami's run-up and horizontal inundation are different. In fact, they may be as little as a few inches in height and distance, as happened on the Japanese islands following the March 31, 2002, earthquake near Taiwan. Nevertheless, these two components of tsunamis are responsible for countless deaths and untold billions of dollars in property losses, and, for the general public, they may be the least understood characteristic of tsunamis.

Before-and-after photos of the Scotch Cap lighthouse in Alaska show the destructive power of a tsunami that struck on April 1, 1946.

Run-Up and Inundation

The key to understanding run-up and inundation distance lies in remembering that tsunamis carry a phenomenal amount of energy and water with them as they hit the shore. In fact, the distances a tsunami's waters travel onshore are often at least twice as great as the height of the water column approaching the shore. Therefore, a tsunami that hits the shore as a two-meter-high wave has a vertical run-up of two meters, but its horizontal inundation distance may exceed four meters. A tsunami of that apparently modest size that hit several Russian islands in the northwestern Pacific in 1975 had waves powerful enough to cause bridge and road damage and destroy fishing settlements.

However, tsunami run-up figures from around the world have been much greater and much more destructive. The 1964 Alaska earthquake sent tsunami waves roaring into the state's bays and fjords; at Whittier, the wave crested at 31.7 meters above the low tide line. The volume of the water of a tsunami run-up is equally important; it can move trees, buildings, ships, and almost anything it encounters. On Kodiak Island, Alaska, the 1964 tsunamis—five in all—moved an eighty-six-foot-long ship five blocks inland and, according to some reports, moved one building over the town jetty not once but four times. Douglas Myles writes,

> The ebbing of the first wave took [the building] over the jetty and out into the bay, according to eyewitnesses. The second wave brought it back in, but again the ebb took it out. Apparently, it was the third wave that brought it to its final "mooring," battered but still whole, perhaps 200 yards from its original Benson Avenue site. [33]

When a tsunami strikes a populated coast, run-up heights and inundation distances can be determined from both post-event surveys and survivor accounts. However, tsunamis have left their mark on landscapes around the world since prehistoric times. Scientists are beginning to recognize the geologic signatures of paleotsunamis, and these ancient events, which had no human

Tsunamis that hit Kodiak Island, Alaska, carried large boats several blocks inland, leaving them stranded.

witnesses, are helping researchers to not only decipher the earth's history but also prepare for what may lie ahead.

Tsunami Signatures

Along the southeast coast of Australia, researchers have found evidence of repeated inundation by tsunamis. These tsunamis seem to have been triggered by landslides in the Tasman Sea, and seem to have occurred on a fairly regular basis. The first tsunami struck roughly seven thousand years ago, and the most recent about eight hundred years ago. According to researchers Edward Bryant and David Price, "The recurrence interval of tsunami[s] is now approaching one event every 600 years,"[34] which suggests that the area might be subjected to another tsunami in the near future. Bryant and Price continue:

> This . . . evidence indicates that the largest tsunami waves swept sediment across the continental shelf . . . with ve-

locities in excess of 10 meters per second. Along cliffs . . . waves reached elevations of 40–100 m. . . . Preliminary evidence on the Shoalhaven [River] delta indicates that waves penetrated 10 km inland for at least one event. This geomorphic evidence suggests that the New South Wales south coast is subject to tsunami waves an order of magnitude greater than that indicated by historic tide gauge records.[35]

Similar research has occurred along the Pacific Northwest coastlines of North America. Independent investigations by Brian Atwater of the USGS, John Adams of the Geological Survey of Canada, and Kenji Satake of the Geological Survey of Japan helped explain geologic features found along coastal estuaries of Washington State and in samples taken from ocean-floor deposits off the northwest coast. The research draws a picture of "at least 12 giant earthquakes along the Cascadia subduction zone [the unstable area that gave rise to the Cascade Mountain range] over the last 7700 years"[36] that have generated tsunamis, the most recent occurring in January 1700. Thanks to meticulous Japanese tsunami records, the researchers "were able to fix the time of the [tsunamigenic] earthquake at about nine in the evening, local time, on January 26, 1700. And on the basis of the size of the tsunami, they were able to estimate the size of the earthquake: it had a magnitude of about 9.0"[37]—in the same range as the 1964 Alaska quake.

This geologic and written evidence indicates that the Pacific Northwest has regularly undergone devastation by tsunamis, but has experienced none in the last three hundred years. The Cascadia subduction zone remains active, and it is not implausible to suggest that one day, another earthquake like that of 1700 will send a tsunami roaring toward the coast. Millions more people live along this coastline today than did in 1700; no one knows for sure how a tsunami event would affect today's seaside communities and populations of Oregon, Washington, and British Columbia. However, there are lessons that can be learned from other heavily populated coastlines that have experienced tsunamis.

Valdivia, Chile, May 22, 1960

On May 22, 1960, fishing captain Georges DeGiorgio was in southern Chile to pick up three newly constructed fishing boats. He was visiting some friends on board the *Isaza,* a flat-bottomed landing craft belonging to the Chilean navy, in the harbor of the town of Corral when a tsunami—the largest tsunami generated by an earthquake that was ever recorded—struck the region. In an interview with the author, DeGiorgio recalled that memorable day.

One of the crew members came to the officers' quarters and said there's something happening with the sea. And we went on deck, and we could see that the water was receding [and] was getting lower and lower . . . until it left us sitting on the bottom. We were at the mouth of the Calle Calle River, so we were really close to the open [Pacific] ocean. . . .

I think [the water] must have gone out at least five meters because there were a couple of German ships [in the harbor as well], and they heeled over [on their sides] quite a bit. The one closest to us was the *Haverbeck* . . . and pretty soon we saw men getting off the ship. We could see them climbing over the rail . . . and try to walk towards Corral. We could see that the crew had only gone a few yards because of the mud—they were up to their knees in this—sucked up by the wet mud—and they never reached shore. They didn't even make it halfway to shore. I would say they were able to go maybe a hundred yards and that was it, and the water came in, and it drowned every one of them.

We were so worried about this whole situation that I don't know how much time passed before the water came back. But the water came back—and I wouldn't say it came back like a big wave or anything; it just came back as a very rapid rise. . . . The *Isaza* was . . . a very easy to maneuver ship . . . but the water picked us up, and first of all, it pushed us immediately inland—and no maneuvering possible—we were completely out of control. . . . The water rose and rose and rose and it took us upstream, up the river, swirling, going around in circles . . . and then we started seeing trees, and barns, and cows and cattle, that the water was pushing us past—a lot of destruction.

And you're not paying attention to how long this took. After a while, about maybe five kilometers from where we started, . . . the water started receding again, and we were in the middle of fields that had been some farm.

Hokkaido, Japan, July 12, 1993

On July 12, 1993, a strong earthquake occurred in the Sea of Japan off the west coast of the northern Japanese island of Hokkaido. The quake had a magnitude of 7.8 and was widely felt throughout the region, including the northern end of Honshu Island. Okushiri Island, off the Hokkaido coast, was struck by a tsunami approximately five minutes after the earthquake ceased.

Okushiri Island was inundated by waves from 5 to 12 meters tall, with a maximum run-up height of 31.5 meters recorded in a small area along the island's southwest coast. Earthquake engineer Peter Yanev, who visited a village on the island two weeks later, made this report:

> In Aonae (population about 1,500), half of the 690 houses were washed away by tsunamis even though most were bounded by recently constructed, massive concrete tsunami walls. Generally, the damage to wood-frame buildings nearest the coast was total. Many concrete foundations could be

Small boats and a rooftop rest on rubble after the seaside port on Okushiri Island, off the Japanese coast, was flattened by tsunamis on July 12, 1993.

seen afterwards with sill anchor bolts but without a shred of wood—either sills or vertical framing. Several concrete and steel buildings were also damaged. [38]

Okushiri Island's port facilities were heavily damaged, and all power lines for several miles along the island's west coast were destroyed. The tsunamis stripped many roads of their concrete pavement and washed the material far inland. More than two hundred people died in this lightly populated resort area. Yanev's report included these comments on the effectiveness of the island's tsunami walls:

> Typically, the settled coast of Okushiri was bounded by recently constructed tsunami walls, which ranged up to about 4.5 [meters] high. . . . The southernmost part of Aonae was completely surrounded by such a wall. The tsunami washed right over the wall and destroyed all wood-frame structures in the area. The tsunami wall may have been partially effective in slowing down and moderating the height of the tsunami but it was ineffective (in this, as well as other areas) in protecting people and property. [39]

Learning from Each Tsunami

The Hokkaido tsunami is a stark reminder that tsunamis can strike quickly and cause extensive damage and loss of life, even in areas that have experienced tsunamis in the past and also taken precautions to minimize their impact. As scientists learn more about how tsunamis are affected by the area where they are generated, how they interact with the offshore bathymetry, and how they behave when they strike, both researchers and civil officials will be able to better understand the areas most at risk around the world. Post-tsunami studies continue to yield valuable information about run-up and inundation levels, which in turn are helping scientists to refine their tsunami models. All of this is essential in order to help coastal communities prepare for and react to the next tsunami.

In the Waves' Wake

A fter the last of the tsunami wave train has receded from the coastline, survivors of the phenomenon try to assess the waves' effects. In most cases, those who have experienced a tsunami immediately try to determine if there have been any injuries or fatalities among their community. However, in many cases, survivors are primarily concerned with the basics of staying alive until help arrives. In some cases, help arrives quickly. In other cases, it may take days.

Waiting for Help in Valdivia, Chile, 1960

In the wake of the tsunami that hit Valdivia, Chile, on May 22, 1960, residents were faced with a landscape that not only had been inundated by the tsunami but had been changed irrevocably. In most tsunami events, the waves crash onto the shore and eventually subside back into the sea. But the earthquakes that had preceded the Valdivia tsunami had caused parts of the city of Valdivia to sink from two to four meters in a process geologists call subsidence. This meant that when the tsunami hit, the areas that had been flooded stayed flooded. According to an eyewitness account, the waters "had covered the first floor [and had reached] the second floor of almost every house and building"[40] in town, forcing the residents to seek higher ground in the hills surrounding Valdivia, where they waited out the aftershocks and hoped help was on its way.

Because of the geologic events that precede most tsunamis, however, help takes time to arrive. Aid may be delayed by damaged roads, and communication outages may prevent hard-hit areas from summoning emergency assistance. Valdivia was cut off from the rest of Chile except by the sea, as the area roads and railroads were unusable. It took several days for the first scouting parties to reach Valdivia, and it was more than a week before medical and welfare personnel arrived.

Valdivia was not the only area affected. Other communities in Chile also experienced earthquakes, subsidence, and tsunamis on May 22. Tsunamis devastated other areas of the Chilean coastline, and like ripples in a pond, they also raced out across the Pacific Ocean to the west and south, traveling hundreds of miles an hour. Fifteen hours after the first tsunamis hit Chile, other waves struck Hawaii, devastating Hilo's waterfront. Japan was hit seven hours after that, catching many by surprise and destroying five thousand homes along the coasts of Honshu and Hokkaido islands. Both urban and sparsely populated areas were affected, and emergency response times were largely determined not only by where help was needed but also by how prepared emergency officials were to deal with such a disaster.

Residents of Valdivia, Chile, walk through their damaged city a few days after the destructive earthquake and tsunami hit on May 22, 1960.

Are Emergency Officials Prepared?

The severity of the 1960 tsunami sent a message to emergency officials concerning their communities' disaster preparations. They realized that they needed to improve their ability to respond to tsunamis. By 1960, scientists understood enough about tsunamis to be able to predict when and where they might strike following a seismic event. In fact, according to Edward Bryant, the tsunami's arrival time at Hilo "was predicted to within a minute"[41] of when it actually struck. However, less than 50 percent of the residents in the target area evacuated. Many people refused to believe the danger the waves posed and the warnings of emergency officials. Three waves hit Hilo, reaching a maximum run-up of almost eleven meters, and killed sixty-one people; many of these victims had gone to the water's edge to watch the tsunami arrive.

After the event, emergency officials gathered to assess the damage and aid the injured. Organizations and government agencies tried to help those who had been affected by the tsunamis. The Red Cross, for example, assisted more than five hundred families affected by the waves, providing them with food, clothing, and shelter. This was a noteworthy accomplishment for the organization, as it was still assisting families who had been made homeless by an eruption of the Kilauea volcano just four months earlier.

The devastation and loss of life associated with the 1960 tsunamis also pointed out to emergency officials that they needed to have greater access to accurate information in order to be better prepared. Although areas across the Pacific Ocean were warned that tsunamis might be heading their way, many individuals and organizations were caught unprepared for the waves' onslaught and particularly for their aftermath. To improve tsunami awareness, the Intergovernmental Oceanographic Commission (IOC) of the United Nations established the International Tsunami Information Center (ITIC) in 1968. The ITIC's mission is to address the information needs of the members of the international tsunami warning network. From its offices in Honolulu, Hawaii, the ITIC works to develop ties to scientific and cultural organizations, emergency preparedness organizations, and the general public throughout the Pacific basin. The center maintains a library to disseminate tsunami knowledge and works with nations to develop local tsunami warning systems, preparedness activities, and response guidelines.

All this groundwork is paying off. Emergency officials around the world are increasingly aware of tsunamigenic conditions and how to deal with the potential for a tsunami strike and any possible conditions in the tsunamis' aftermath. For example, when earthquakes hit western Japan in 1993, the firefighters of Okushiri Island's small town of Aonae realized immediately that their services might soon be required. According to Peter Yanev,

> Shortly after the earthquake, personnel from the 38-person fire department made a quick circuit of the town looking for fires. Seeing none and concerned about tsunami[s], the fire fighters returned to the fire station, which is on top of a bluff, to await the need for emergency service.[42]

Had this small firefighting team been unaware of the possibility of a tsunami, they might have been caught at the waterfront when the waves hit. But because they were well educated about a type of disaster characteristic of their region, they were back at their post and were able to respond to a fire that swept through Aonae, fueled in part by the ruptured fuel tanks of fishing boats the tsunamis threw ashore.

Not all areas in the path of tsunamis are as well prepared as Aonae. Thus when tsunami wave trains strike communities whose police, firefighters, and emergency medical personnel lack the training necessary to mount an effective response, the populations must carry on the best they can until help arrives. Fortunately, however, significant improvements have been made in developing tsunami readiness and response procedures.

Disaster Relief Efforts in Remote Areas

Worldwide communications have improved tremendously since the May 1960 tsunamis in the Pacific. In 1960, many people around the world did not learn about the disasters until they read newspapers a day after the initial earthquakes and tsunamis in Chile. Before the newspapers carried early wire-service accounts of the catastrophe in Valdivia, Hawaii and Japan had also been struck by tsunamis.

Parking meters in Hilo, Hawaii, were flattened by the force of debris-filled tsunamis generated by the earthquake that struck Valdivia, Chile.

However, by the time of the 1998 Papua New Guinea tsunami, improvements in communications networks, as well as the development of the Internet, had made news reporting almost instantaneous. Whereas residents of Valdivia, Chile, had to wait for almost two weeks for help to arrive in force, today emergency agencies are better organized and better prepared to launch relief efforts quickly.

The relief efforts associated with the Papua New Guinea tsunami are an example of the increased speed with which aid can be given. The tsunami struck on a Friday evening. The victims were first discovered the following morning (Saturday). By Monday, two evaluation teams from the International Federation of Red Cross and Red Crescent Societies (IFRC) had begun coordinating a relief operation with the Papua New Guinea Red Cross. A news report issued four days after the tsunamis struck documents the speed at which aid can now arrive at even a remote are:

> One team, made up of IFRC members and two international delegates, departed Bougainville, an island northeast of Papua New Guinea where relief workers had been assisting

Site Surveys

Tsunami researchers visit the site of a tsunami strike as soon after the strike as possible in order to collect data before the clean-up process begins. Once restoration efforts are well under way, evidence of run-up and inundation conditions is obscured or obliterated. Researchers from the University of Southern California joined other scientists at the Papua New Guinea sites two weeks after the tsunami hit in July 1998. Professor Costas Synolakis reported daily on the team's ship-borne surveys and their observations of the tsunami's aftermath. His comments are found on the USC Tsunami Research Group's website and are excerpted below.

August 3, 1998—The survey began in Aitape, 2 runup points were measured of over 3m each. We were given permission to enter Sissano lagoon and measured 10m runups and wave height. The damage is extensive. The entire lagoon is full of debris. Media reports of damage around Sissano lagoon were not exaggerated. Overland flow depth of 12m were recorded. Entire place has been swept clean by the wave, leaving only trees. We explored the lagoon by boat and damage is extensive. . . .

August 4, 1998—We continued to survey the Sissano lagoon area, this time venturing to the west side of the lagoon and main village. Water flow depths of over 5m were recorded at 400m inland. All buildings were destroyed. The day also included several helicopter sorties over the affected area. From this vantage point, we were able to see the extreme inundation. In the afternoon, another point was surveyed about 8km to the west and here we also found evidence of 7m flow depth on the beach.

drought victims; and the other [team] is a Papua New Guinea Red Cross team that left Port Moresby.

IFRC relief supplies will arrive as well, sent by boat on a two-day sail out of Lae, located on Papua New Guinea's north coast.

The IFRC is sending clothes, shelter materials, medicines, water and building tools for future construction efforts, said Marie-Francoise Borel, an IFRC spokesperson. "Our focus is on helping the survivors, help them rebuild their homes, help them get their lives together."

Australia dispatched three Royal Australian Air Force C-130 transports carrying supplies. The first arrived at Vanimo on Monday morning, equipped with a field hospital and a team of doctors, nurses and engineers. New Zealand plans to send medical teams to Papua New Guinea on Monday or Tuesday.[43]

Over the next several weeks, more and more relief teams and supplies arrived in the stricken areas. After the first few hectic days, medical personnel saw fewer and fewer emergencies, but they started to be concerned about the possibility of disease. As time passed, survivors began to show signs of influenza, pneumonia, malaria, and cholera. This was to be expected, for diseases spread quickly in damp, crowded environments, and in Papua New Guinea, survivors had to be put in temporary housing in close quarters. According to Dr. Michael McGeehin, chief of the health studies division at the Centers for Disease Control and Prevention in Atlanta, Georgia,

A search-and-rescue team from Florida helps in the rescue effort following the Papua New Guinea tsunami in July 1998.

> One of the most classic ways of disease developing in a situation like that relates to the basic public health, basic water and sanitation. You'll have displaced people and you'll have sanitation issues and water possibly becoming contaminated through human waste. The water that people are drinking becomes impacted and people consume the water and become ill.[44]

Aid workers strive to identify, isolate, and treat people who develop disease in hopes of preventing it from spreading throughout the temporary camps and to other populations in the area. In some cases, the local or national government of the stricken area will quarantine the camps and the areas of worst impact until health officials and emergency response teams have determined that the threat of disease has passed.

In the immediate aftermath of any crisis, relief workers aid the injured, identify the victims, and assess and deal with the threat of disease. They try to reunite families, although, occasionally, some family members may have died. Once that phase has passed, relief agencies scale back their efforts as families try to rebuild shattered lives and communities address the need to rebuild destroyed infrastructure. This hard work involves long-term commitment and careful planning, and requires cooperation between local, national, and often international agencies.

Dealing with the Crisis and the Loss

Any sort of disaster leaves an impact on the emotional well-being of its victims. Though a traumatic event may have been experienced by thousands of people, no two individuals will be affected in the same way. Some may be able to deal with the catastrophe and move on, attempting to rebuild their lives while putting the past behind them. Others may feel that they have come to terms with the event but then discover that weeks, months, or even years later something—a smell, a sound, or a picture—will bring it all flooding back. Some victims of the 1960 Chilean tsunamis, interviewed more than thirty years later, re-created their actions and reactions that day. According to the government circular *Surviving a Tsunami,* Estalino Hernandez "climbed an arrayan tree to escape the tsunami's waves. While he clung to the tree, the waters of the tsunami rose to his waist."[45] A few miles away, Ramon Ramirez directed researchers in 1999 to the still standing cypress tree he climbed to escape the tsunami. More than forty years after the event, Georges DeGiorgio can recall the smell of the mud when the waters retreated during the depression wave, as well as some of the first relief supplies to reach Valdivia: "I still remember the cheese, the blankets, and the powdered milk. I ate a lot of cheese."[46]

As food, shelter, and medical concerns begin to decrease from crisis proportions and life begins to return to normal, community leaders must face longer-term choices. Both densely and

In the Aftermath, Unexpected Benefits

Papua New Guinea is home to approximately eight hundred languages, many of which have no written form. In the aftermath of the 1998 tsunami, a project that had been working to create alphabets for some of the area languages suddenly found new life and new participants. Wycliffe International, a nondenominational group of Bible translators based in Florida, is a partner in the translation project. Their report, "Swept Away," written three years after the tsunami, documents some of the changes.

> As word spread throughout the surrounding communities that Arop would be hosting translation and literacy workshops, more and more language groups have asked to be included in the Aitape West Translation Project. . . .

> During an alphabet development workshop, new delegates from nine languages and dialects created their own alphabet for the first time. For many participants it was a lifelong dream to see their language in written form. . . .

> The long-awaited multi-language translation workshop was held September 24–October 12, 2001. . . . Joachim Ali arrived in Arop the day before the alphabet workshop started. Joachim is a speaker of the Ulau language, a coastal language located east of Aitape, about a five-hour drive away. Since the Aitape West Translation Project targets the western language groups, no information had been sent to anyone from Joachim's language group or any of the others in that area.

> But reports of the upcoming workshop had reached Ulau, and they had decided to send their best man—Joachim. The Ulau people needed an alphabet to set up a kindergarten in their language, so Joachim asked if he could participate in the workshop.

> There he produced a first draft of an Ulau alphabet.

lightly populated communities need to make tough decisions about what to do with the areas that suffered the most damage. Elected officials receive input from both residents and scientists who studied the waves' impacts. Their decisions can determine the community's direction in the tsunamis' aftermath.

Coping with Catastrophic Change

In the wake of a tsunami, a community may be changed slightly, substantially, or completely. Some residents may wish to return to rebuild immediately; others may prefer to study their options first. All such decisions can affect the area's response to future tsunamis.

Some communities, like Valdivia, have no alternative but to confront the reality of major change. When parts of the Chilean coastal city were flooded in 1960, it was obvious immediately that the community would never be exactly the same. Now, over forty years later, visitors to Valdivia can tour a city that has taken advantage of the changes inflicted by the disaster. For example, tourists today can take boat tours of the stricken areas and see the remnants of flooded buildings and landmarks, and can stroll along Costanera Avenue, which, according to one writer, "affords one the opportunity to enjoy views from the Calle Calle and Pedro de Valdivia bridges. The combination of calm water, beautiful gardens and tourist and cargo boats . . . transform it into a gorgeous place"[47] for visitors.

Deciding Not to Rebuild

Hilo and Aonae chose different paths. These communities did not undergo overwhelming change, like Valdivia did, but recognizing that tsunamis may strike again, they wanted to learn from the past. Hilo's waterfront has been battered twice by tsunamis; the 1960 event destroyed an area that had been rebuilt after a similar disaster less than twenty years earlier. After extensive study, Hawaiian and federal government officials decided not to rebuild along the waterfront.

Today, areas that were devastated in the mid-twentieth century are mostly open parkland. Buildings immediately adjacent to this buffer zone must meet strict building codes for their ability to withstand potential tsunamis. The Hilo Community Development Plan specifies that

buildings should be designed so that a tsunami will pass under them or wash through areas not intended for human occupancy; . . . buildings should be oriented to present their narrowest sides to a tsunami; . . . buildings should be sited on the highest natural elevation of their lot and earth platforms to gain foundation elevation.[48]

All of these rules are designed to reduce potential property damage in the aftermath of the next tsunami.

Rebuilding to Enhance Protection

Hilo had considered constructing seawalls and breakwaters after both the 1946 and 1960 tsunamis but decided against them because of aesthetic reasons. Aonae, on the other hand, already had a seawall in place when the 1993 tsunami hit; since then, the island community has increased the seawall's height from 4.5 meters to 11 meters in order to try to reduce further damage in the wake of future tsunamis.

The coastal city of Valdivia, Chile, has been rebuilt and tourists can now take boat tours to view flooded buildings and other landmarks left in the wake of the tsunami.

Tsunamis' Hidden Costs

Each community affected by tsunamis makes difficult decisions in the aftermath of the waves. For some communities, however, the aftermath may have caused ecological damage that has the potential to lead to a social disruption that no rebuilding process can repair.

After any disaster, someone will inevitably total up the cost of the crisis. Reports will be written, statistics compiled, and press releases issued, all counting up the dollars it will take to rebuild a community or to feed and house the victims. Yet little attention is paid to what happens when former residents who wish to return to their pretsunami occupations are unable to do so because of the waves' destruction.

Such hidden costs may depend on how long it takes for the environment to recover. Coastal communities often rely heavily on industries connected to the sea, such as fishing or shell fishing, and these vital resources may have been adversely affected by the tsunamis themselves or by the damage associated with them. In the wake of the 1964 Alaskan tsunamis, the state's crab fishing industry was virtually shut down for nine months until the crab population rebounded. A similar crisis today would affect far more than the local fishing industry, because Alaskan fishermen sell their catches all over the world. In addition, given the expansion of the crab fishing fleet since 1964, the potential exists for significant environmental damage.

Costs related to tsunamis go far beyond property damage such as this in Kodiak, Alaska, to include destruction of economic resources like local fisheries.

The 1993 tsunami that struck Okushiri Island sent fishing vessels crashing over the seawall at Aonae, smashing their hulls, dumping fuel oil into the rampaging waters, and causing unknown amounts of environmental damage. By the time the fishing fleet was rebuilt, at least some marine populations seem to have recovered, but longer-term effects of the oil spills may not show up for years. After the 1998 tsunami, Papua New Guinea's fishermen were affected not only by environmental damage to the fisheries in Sissano Lagoon but also by changes in their own psychological makeup. Many reported feeling reluctant to go out to sea after the tsunamis for fear of returning and finding that they would have to deal with the aftermath of yet another tsunami.

Learning from the Past, Preparing for the Future

Communities around the world have learned to deal with the aftermath of tsunamis. Some areas, such as Japan, bring to the task a resolve born of centuries-long cultural experience with such disasters. Other populations, with few recorded instances of tsunamis, are less accustomed to their dangers, effects, and aftermath, although they live in areas where the land speaks of past inundations. As scientific and governmental communities become more connected, they share more information about tsunamis. With each newly recorded instance, and with each new geologic investigation, vulnerable populations learn more and more about what to expect and how to lessen tsunamis' potential destruction.

Watching the Waters

I nevitably, in the aftermath of a tsunami, people who live along the world's coastlines begin to wonder whether the devastated areas could be struck again, and whether such a disaster could happen where they live. Scientists are now beginning to understand that the answer to both questions is a resounding "yes." Even areas that were considered relatively safe because they were not subject to regular seismic activity are now drawing attention. In addition, the studies of the tsunamis that struck Nicaragua in 1992 and Papua New Guinea in 1998 have led scientists to a greater understanding of tsunamigenic conditions and, perhaps more important, how to anticipate these conditions in the future.

Foreseeing the Future

One of the challenges with foreseeing any future tsunamis lies in being able to anticipate the triggering events. Currently, scientists are unable to predict tsunamigenic occurrences such as earthquakes, landslides, and volcanic eruptions, although volcanologists have had some recent success in this area. Instead of trying to predict the future, researchers rely on identifying areas in which complex geologic conditions might indicate susceptibility to tsunamis. Tsunami scientists also realize that, since they are unable to prevent changes in the geological makeup of the planet, perhaps the best way to deal with the unpredictable events of the future is to be as prepared as possible when the triggers occur.

Tsunamis have the potential to strike coastlines after a triggering event occurs hundreds or even thousands of miles away. As the tsunami waves radiate out like ripples in a pond, they have the potential to wreak havoc in a 360-degree arc around the event's location. While communities on distant coastlines may have as long as twenty-four hours to prepare for the onrushing waves, those people living close to the tsunamigenic source seldom have more than thirty minutes. The 1946 Aleutian tsunamis slammed in Unimak Island only twenty-one minutes after the earthquake that launched them. The next time Alaska was hit, in 1964, earthquakes were followed by tsunamis almost immediately, which meant that for some residents there was no time for a warning.

Nearfield and Farfield

Scientists divide tsunamis into two types: Nearfield tsunamis are those that are triggered by local events, and farfield tsunamis are those that occur based on events that took place at a distance from where the tsunamis struck. Thus, the 1946 nearfield tsunami that came so quickly upon Alaska residents became a farfield tsunami to Japanese coastal populations, which also suffered.

Currently, nearfield tsunamis are the greatest concern for scientists wishing to foresee future tsunamigenic conditions. Nearfield tsunamis in Nicaragua in 1992 and in Papua New Guinea in 1998 puzzled researchers because the run-up and inundation were greater than anticipated. However, they have discovered that the key to these tsunamis was not the earthquakes that caught the attention of local residents but the landslides, or slumps, that occurred following the quakes—unseen and unanticipated—somewhere just offshore from where the tsunamis eventually struck. These slumps have led to a revelation about tsunamis and the role that offshore bathymetry plays in future tsunamis. Douglas L. Smith explains what scientists have discovered about these landslides:

El Tranisto, Nicaragua, after a nearfield tsunami in 1992. Earthquakes and a relatively small first wave alerted residents, enabling most to move to safety before larger waves destroyed the village.

This large rock was carried fifty meters inland by a tsunami, demonstrating the power such waves carry.

The slump creates a void behind itself that the water rushes into, so that if it's moving towards deeper water the depression wave points towards land. [USC's Costas] Synolakis says, "So finally we have a model that corroborates eyewitness accounts. In every tsunami in the past eight years, people always say the sea withdrew first, and then the wave came. Before Papua New Guinea, we could only try to explain this in terms of tectonic tsunamis, but now we know why. Unfortunately, the model shows that if you put the trough first, you get double the run-up than if you put the crest first."[49]

These new findings have prompted renewed interest by university researchers and U.S. government agencies to examine the coastal areas of the nation to identify areas that show past slumping and which may be susceptible to it in the future. The U.S. Geological Survey recently released a map of the seafloor off Santa Monica Bay, California, that revealed "evidence that in the past large mass movements have occurred in the bay, suggesting that they may well happen again in the future."[50] Such a slump could generate a nearfield tsunami that could hit the area almost immediately, giving residents little time to evacuate. Clearly, the time to prepare for a future tsunami is before the threat of one occurs.

Preparing for future tsunamis depends on whether the tsunami is likely to be a nearfield or a farfield event. While residents of the "big island" of Hawaii would have more time to prepare for a wave train in the event of tsunamigenic conditions off the coast of South America, they would have considerably less time if an unexpected coastal landslide from the island into the neighboring sea resulted in tsunamis almost immediately. So, the scientific community and governmental agencies are working together to educate citizens on how to prepare for a tsunami strike with as little as ten minutes' warning.

Evolving Warning Systems

Following the 1960 Chilean and 1964 Alaskan earthquakes, the United Nations worked with the international scientific communities to establish the International Coordination Group for Tsunami Warning System in the Pacific (called ITSU) to observe and report seismic activity and sea-level change throughout the Pacific basin. Today, thirty-five nations and territories belong to the system and receive tsunami watches and warnings from the Pacific Tsunami Warning Center (PTWC) in Hawaii. Tsunami watches and warnings are similar to severe weather alerts; a watch means that an underwater earthquake sizable enough to generate a tsunami has occurred, and a warning is issued when a tide station records a disturbance. A tsunami warning issued by the PTWC has the function of "alerting warning system participants to the approach of a potentially destructive tsunami and repeating tsunami times of arrival for all locations."[51]

The track record of existing tsunami warning systems is not impressively accurate, however. According to Edward Bryant, "75% of tsunami warnings since 1950 have resulted in erroneous alarms."[52] An evacuation ordered in 1986 for Honolulu for an expected tsunami that never materialized cost more than $30 million in economic losses. Part of the problem lies in the unpredictable nature of tsunamis; they may form when scientists do not expect them, or they may fail to materialize under the most typical tsunamigenic conditions. However, evolving technology is creating optimism that

The 1964 tsunamis in Alaska were strong enough to drive a wooden plank through this truck tire.

warning centers will soon be able to broadcast effective and accurate alerts for both farfield and nearfield tsunamis.

One project, called Deep-Ocean Assessment and Reporting of Tsunamis (DART), seeks to reduce "the loss of lives and property in U.S. coastal communities" and to eliminate "false alarms and the high economic cost of unnecessary evacuations."[53] DART currently collects seismic information from sensors placed on the seafloor. These sensors are so sensitive that they can detect a tsunami with an amplitude as small as one centimeter. They are connected to a moored buoy that transmits information in real time via a geostationary satellite. Currently, NOAA has six of these sensors in place in the Pacific, and hopes to have five more

Buoys like this one collect seismic information from sensors that can detect even the smallest tsunamis and then transmit the data to researchers. With such developing technology, scientists hope to be able to predict tsunamis.

in place by 2003. The sensors are placed in areas that have historically been associated with tsunamigenic activity, but they have not yet been put to the test by triggering conditions.

Officials project that, when complete, this system will be linked to state-of-the-art tsunami models that will be able to accurately predict where a tsunami will strike, as well as run-up and inundation expectations. All of this information will be transmitted to emergency officials and the general public through broadcast networks such as NOAA's National Weather Service alert system and the U.S. Coast Guard's marine alert system. But what the public does with this information is contingent on effective education.

Education and Preparation for the Future

The challenge for emergency preparedness agencies is to disseminate life-saving information as widely as possible. Experts agree that when a tsunami warning is issued, the most prudent course of action is to leave the shoreline and head toward higher ground inland. If that is not feasible, people are advised to assemble on the upper floors of sturdy buildings. Emergency officials hope to educate the public so that, in future tsunami emergencies, the populations at risk can be evacuated with as few mishaps as possible.

Education efforts may take many forms, such as lectures, demonstrations, drills, and publications. One such publication, *Tsunami Warning!,* is a richly illustrated book directed primarily to Hawaiian children, but its messages apply to all who may find themselves faced with tsunamis in the future. The book reinforces the message that getting as far away from the coast is the best course of action:

> As soon as the [earthquake] shaking stops, people living by sea do not start to clean up the mess. They quickly leave their homes and move inland away from the sea. They know that earthquakes can trigger off tsunami waves. . . .
>
> There isn't much time. People hurry to safety, away from the shore and wait for the tsunami to come. [54]

This, of course, is more easily said than done. Accidents and injuries may be inevitable if, for example, it becomes necessary to evacuate thousands of people from a crowded Southern California beach on a sunny Saturday afternoon. However, a recent event across the Pacific Ocean from California gives scientists hope for nearfield tsunami survival.

A Possible Catastrophe Averted

One of the greatest success stories related to the efforts of the ITIC and similar agencies involved in tsunami education occurred on the small island nation of Vanuatu in the Pacific Ocean. Using the lessons learned from the tsunamis of the last decade, UNESCO created a video about volcanoes, earthquakes, and tsunamis, and local authorities carried it, along with a television and a portable generator, to every village throughout the islands. The video described the Papua New Guinea disaster and warned villagers to run for high ground if they felt the ground shaking or saw the water receding.

On November 26, 1999, villagers at Bai Mairtele on Pentecost Island felt the earth shake and saw the water recede. According to Douglas L. Smith,

> As it happened, the ground shaking . . . was not very strong, but they saw the water receding. There was a nearby hill, and they all ran up it. And stayed there. That's the big lesson—slumps can happen quite some time after the main shock, so [the tsunami researchers] tell them to stay away for half an hour to an hour. It has happened in the past that a wave comes in and people run; then they return to look for loved ones or survey the damage, and they get hit by the second wave. Or the third wave.[55]

This nearfield tsunami, which had a run-up of at least eight meters at Bai Mairtele and which may have been triggered by an offshore landslide, inflicted heavy damage and casualties elsewhere across Pentecost Island. But at Bai Mairtele, only three people died. According to Costas Synolakis, this was "amazing. . . . Of all the science we did, this was the best part. It really did save lives."[56]

Saving lives remains the overall goal of anyone involved in tsunami science. From the mathematician who develops computer models of theoretical run-up and inundation depths, to the field geologist who visits the sites of tsunami damage to assess what happened, to the emergency officials and aid workers who strive to return lives to normal, each is working to ensure that the next tsunami does not catch target areas unaware and unprepared.

However, the key to dealing with disasters is more than just education and preparation; anticipation also must play a role. This is particularly important when dealing with tsunamis, since run-up

What If an Asteroid Hit the Earth Today?

Although the vast majority of tsunamis are generated by terrestrial activity, the threat of waves generated by extraterrestrial impacts still exists. In the past few years, several small meteorites have burned up in the earth's atmosphere. They provide exciting light shows to the general public but are a source of concern for some individuals who fear that we would be unprepared to deal with the potential impact of a larger space object. Leonard David, the senior space writer for Space.com, reports that scientists are studying what might happen today if a large asteroid or comet hit the earth's oceans. In "Asteroid Busting: We Have the Technology" (published on the Space.com website), he quotes a scientist who paints an alarming picture.

"Plunking down in ocean waters, an asteroid measuring several kilometers across would churn up frightening tsunami conditions," said Jack Hills, a researcher at Los Alamos National Laboratory.

For example, given an impact far out in the Pacific Ocean, those along the California coastline might have several hours of time for fleeing to higher ground. But on the Atlantic coast, with high mountains far from shore, the situation is perilous.

"Long Island would be totally hosed," Hills said. "I'm not sure people should have been allowed to build there, not just because of any asteroid impact threat but even from storm surges. If something occurred today, it would cause over $100 billion in damage on Long Island," he said.

and inundation conditions are difficult to predict. Therefore, emergency officials base their preparations on the worst-case scenarios and anticipate that the largest expected wave for given conditions and locations will actually occur. These estimates are only as good as the scientific information at hand.

Experimentation and Evaluation

At research centers around the world, scientists are working to improve their understanding of tsunamis. Much of this study involves combining analysis of previous events with computer-generated models of areas that may experience tsunamis in the future. For example, Stephan Grilli, an ocean engineering professor at the University of Rhode Island, is taking advantage of recent observations that 60 percent of all major tsunamis are caused by a combination of earthquake and landslide events. Recognizing that ocean bathymetry also plays a role, Grilli says, "In an unstable area where there are large accumulations of sediment, like along the continental shelf, an earthquake could cause a major landslide. And that combination of events can cause huge tsunamis."[57]

Grilli uses a thirty-meter wave tank to better understand landslides and tsunamis and is developing several computer models based on previous computer work and his wave-tank simulations. One model will examine how sediments move when struck by earthquakes, and another will focus on the resulting behavior of the overlying water. A third will attempt to predict run-up and inundation levels from these waves. Grilli hopes that these tsunami prediction models will aid community efforts to assess and alleviate potentially hazardous areas and situations. He says, "If you can predict where [tsunamis] are most likely to occur and predict their intensity and speed, then you can mitigate potential damage."[58]

The process of damage mitigation—analyzing, understanding, and reducing the potential for losses of property and life—is gaining increased attention, particularly along the west coast of the United States. In this region, tsunami risk awareness has grown in the last ten years, based in part on the experiences of

Honduras and Papua New Guinea. In response, NOAA, USGS, the National Science Foundation, and the Federal Emergency Management Agency fostered partnerships with state and local officials and members of the scientific community to form the National Tsunami Hazard Mitigation Program in 1996.

In March 2002, the program issued "Designing for Tsunamis: Seven Principles for Planning and Designing for Tsunami Hazards," a no-nonsense guide to dealing with tsunami-related issues, such as understanding risks to a community, reducing tsunami risks in new construction, improving existing structures, and developing evacuation strategies. The guide points out that, although tsunamis have hit the western United States six times since 1946,

many communities at risk in the Pacific region have no recent experience with tsunami damage and, hence, may have a false sense of security regarding the hazard.

An estimated 489 cities within the Pacific states of Alaska, California, Hawaii, Oregon and Washington are susceptible to tsunamis; as many as 900,000 residents of these cities would be inundated by a 50-foot tsunami.[59]

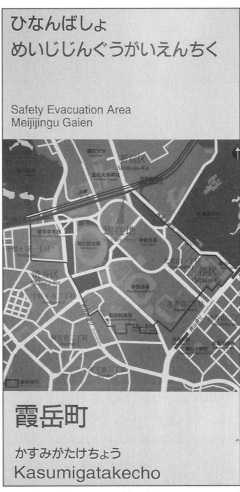

In Tokyo, Japan, maps like this one are posted throughout the city to show evacuation routes in the event of an earthquake or tsunami.

A fifty-foot (fifteen-meter) tsunami hit the west coast of the United States in the recent past, and a recurrence is not out of the question. During the 1964 tsunamis in Alaska, maximum run-up in Whittier reached 31.7 meters. Thus, many coastal populations of the United States need to assess their communities and their

Tsunamis at Lake Tahoe

Lake Tahoe, California, is a popular tourist resort. Vacationers and visitors are drawn to the scenic lake and the majestic mountain backdrop. But scientists are discovering that the tranquil scene may have both a tumultuous past and a forbidding future, all because of a recently discovered fault system and seismic evidence in the area. Geologists speculate that debris found at the bottom of the lake reveals that one wall of the lake collapsed within the last ten thousand years, and it may happen again.

Kathryn Brown, writing for Science News Online, projects what might happen if an earthquake of 7 or more on the Richter scale was to move part of the lake floor by four meters:

> According to one [computer-simulation] scenario, a quake along the fault under the north end of the lake would send waves up to 6m high racing toward the community of South Lake Tahoe on the southern shore. In a second scenario, a shift in the fault that runs along the lake's west side catapults 10-meter-tall waves into McKinney Bay on the western shore. . . .

> The good news, geologists say, is that a magnitude 7 quake under Lake Tahoe only has a 3 to 4 percent probability of striking in the next 50 years, given the 1,500-year quake-recurrence interval inferred from tremors along the Genoa fault.

emergency plans in order to minimize potential impacts from future tsunamis. Progress is being made; on June 30, 2001, Ocean Shores, Washington, was the first community to earn the West Coast and Alaska Tsunami Warning Center's "TsunamiReady" designation for their planning and preparation efforts. Since then, additional communities, including the Qwinault Indian tribe of Alaska, have achieved the designation. But as of mid-2002, no communities in California, Oregon, or Hawaii have been chosen as "TsunamiReady."

Are You Ready?

Millions of people around the world are at risk from the threat of tsunamis. As more and more people congregate along the earth's coastlines, the chances increase that heavily populated areas will be struck by tsunamis. Building giant seawalls across the face of every coastline that may be vulnerable to tsunamis would be a tremendously expensive, time-consuming endeavor that would most likely devastate both the economy and the environment of the seaside areas. And as the experiences of Okushiri Island demonstrate, having a seawall does not guarantee protection from tsunamis.

If the history of tsunami events around the world teaches anything, it is that communities in both economically developed and economically developing nations and territories are at risk. Some are ready for what may lie ahead and have educated their citizens about the risks tsunamis pose. Whether residents receive the information at age eighty from the first film they have ever seen or at age eight through the modern convenience of the Internet, communication remains the key to preparation. According to Edward Bryant,

> Most people can escape with as little as ten minutes' warning of a tsunami. Along the northern coastline of Papua New Guinea where the July 1998 tsunami had such an impact, people have been encouraged to adopt a tree. . . . Substantial numbers of trees withstood the impact of the tsunami even though it was 15m high. . . . Notches can be cut into trees as toeholds, and people can easily climb a tree and lash themselves to the trunk in a matter of minutes. [60]

These Pacific islanders are now ready if another tsunami arrives. But urban populations may not be so prepared, and this can have dire consequences. Recalling the evidence that the Cascadia Range in the Pacific Northwest seems to have experienced tsunamis every three hundred to five hundred years, with the last one striking in 1700, Richard Eisner is concerned. Eisner is the northern coastal regional administrator for the California Office of Emergency Services and serves on the National Tsunami Hazard Mitigation Program. He says that the threat of tsunamis is "very real. It has occurred in the past. The difficulty we have is that tsunamis are so infrequent that we can't estimate probability of loss. . . . We're learning that we're at greater risk than we thought."[61]

For coastal communities around the world, the risk for tsunamis is real, and the cost of assuming that one's own area will be spared can be catastrophically high. Perhaps Costas Synolakis sums it up the most succinctly when he says, "History has illustrated all too well the tragic impact of tsunamis in regions ill prepared for this demonstration of the Earth's fury."[62]

Conclusion: Peru, June 23, 2001

O n June 23, 2001, a massive earthquake—the largest recorded in thirty-five years—occurred off the southern coast of Peru, triggering a tsunami that slammed into the nearby coast. Tsunamis were also recorded in Chile, Japan, and Hawaii, but the area around Camaña, Peru, was the hardest hit. The tsunami wave train consisted of four waves, and eyewitnesses recounted that the second and third waves were the largest. Scientists who visited the area later measured the maximum run-up at over eight meters, and the maximum inundation was 760 meters.

The area's population was relatively lucky. The tsunami struck during midafternoon, so many saw the water recede and evacuated immediately. It also struck during the Southern Hemisphere's winter, so fortunately the local beaches were relatively deserted. Although thousands of homes and businesses were destroyed and twenty people lost their lives, the death toll and property losses could have been much greater if the tsunami had struck during the Peruvian summer "when the beach discotheques, hotels and cafes [are] full."[63]

One member of the International Tsunami Survey team sent to Peru writes that most of the residents interviewed "knew what tsunamis were, [and] recognized the water draw down as a sign of danger."[64] and left the area. However, eyewitness accounts demonstrate that tsunami awareness efforts that have been so effective elsewhere have not reached everyone where tsunamis may strike. American Red Cross International Disaster relief worker Andrea Munzer described the situation in Camaña a few days after the tsunamis struck:

> The tsunami completely destroyed homes and crops throughout the town. Metal doors were bent in half from the sheer power of the water. The townspeople still reel from the shock of the disaster. Looking for help, they wandered among relief workers, confused and disoriented, with tears in their eyes and nothing left but the clothes on their backs.

> During the ebb of the initial tide . . . , the water retreated far back from the coast, leaving a wide swath of seafloor exposed. Villagers ran out into the sea to pick up dozens of fish left behind by the powerful recession of the water. But then the tsunami rushed in, overcoming the villagers. . . . "All we heard were screams and then we saw people running, but many could not outrun the wave," described one local.

A woman walks through the remains of Camaña, Peru, which was destroyed in June 2001 by four massive tsunamis.

The first rush of water was followed by two smaller waves, decimating more homes. Salt water settled into the soil, ruining crops and the planting seasons for many years to come.

"I have lost everything, and I don't have anything left," said a local villager. She and her two young children had not eaten in four days. "I don't know what to do." [65]

Although each new tsunami may leave disaster and hardship in its wake, research continues to understand these natural disasters. Scientists and governmental agencies are working to improve communications, education, and protection efforts in order to reduce loss of life and property. However, theirs is a race against time, as no one knows when or where the next tsunamis will strike. And, as history will attest, every coastline is vulnerable; every coast needs to be prepared.

Notes

Introduction: The Aegean Sea, Circa 1450 B.C.

1. Plato, "Timaeus," in *Plato in Twelve Volumes,* trans. R.G. Bury. 1929. Reprint: Cambridge, MA: Harvard University Press, 1975, vol. 9, p. 43.

2. Plato, "Timaeus," vol. 9, p. 43.

3. Spyridon Marinatos, "About the Rumour of Atlantis," quoted in Douglas Myles, *The Great Waves.* New York: McGraw-Hill, 1985, p. 158.

Chapter 1: What Is a Tsunami?

4. Ellen J. Prager, with Kate Hutton, Costas Synolakis, and Stanley Williams, *Furious Earth: The Science and Nature of Earthquakes, Volcanoes, and Tsunamis.* New York: McGraw-Hill, 2000, p. 180.

5. Edward Bryant, *Tsunami: The Underrated Hazard.* Cambridge, England: Cambridge University Press, 2001, p. 178.

6. Quoted in Stephanie Kriner, "Seafloor Landslide Could Push Tsunami Toward U.S. East Coast," May 2000. www.disasterrelief.org.

7. Neal D. Driscoll, Jeffrey K. Weissel, and John D. Goff, "Potential for Large-Scale Submarine Slope Failure and

Tsunami Generation Along the U.S. Mid-Atlantic Coast," *Geology,* May 2000, p. 410.

8. Quoted in Australian Broadcasting Corporation Online, "Transcript, Links, and Further Information for 'Tsunami,'" n.d., p. 1. www.abc.net.au.

9. Bryant, *Tsunami,* p. 245.

10. Myles, *The Great Waves,* p. 57.

11. Quoted in, "Killer Wave, July 20, 1998," *The NewsHour with Jim Lehrer*, p. 2. www.pbs.org.

12. Quoted in, "Killer Wave, July 20, 1998," p. 2.

Chapter 2: A Growing Wave

13. Bryant, *Tsunami,* p. 137.

14. Thomas J. Sokolowski, "West Coast and Alaska Tsunami Warning Center: Mission and Overview," November 2, 2001. http://wcatwc.gov.

15. Bryant, *Tsunami,* p. 220.

16. Daniel Pendick, "Savage Earth. Waves of Destruction: Tsunamis," PBS Online/WNET Thirteen New York, n.d., p. 1. www.pbs.org.

17. Prager et al., *Furious Earth,* p. 172.

18. Alastair Sarre, "Calculating the Threat of Tsunami," *NOVA: Science in the News,* Australian Foundation for Science, p. 1. www.science.org.au.

19. Prager et al., *Furious Earth,* p. 189.

20. Tim Thwaites, "Modelling Tsunami Waves," *Monash Magazine,* February 1998. www.monash.edu.au.

21. National Science Foundation, "NSF Award Abstract—#0086571: Upgrading Oregon State's Multidirectional Wave Basin for Remote Tsunami Research," January 3, 2002. www.fastlane.nsf.gov.

22. National Science Foundation, "NSF Award Abstract—#0086571."

23. King County Office of Emergency Management, Emergency Management Division, Department of Information and

Administrative Services, "Tsunamis and Seiches," part 1, September 24, 1998. www.metrokc.gov.

24. Quoted in CNN.com, "Taiwan Braces for Quake Aftershocks," April 1, 2002. www.cnn.com.

Chapter 3: A Wall of Water

25. Prager et al., *Furious Earth,* p. 165.

26. Bryant, *Tsunami,* p. 10.

27. Prager et al., *Furious Earth,* p. 166.

28. Quoted in Douglas L. Smith, "Of Landslides, Couch Potatoes, and Pocket Tsunamis," *Engineering & Science,* no. 1, 2000, p. 35.

29. U.S. Geological Survey—Western Region Coastal and Marine Geology, "Life of a Tsunami," June 28, 1999. http://walrus.wr.usgs.gov.

30. Smith, "Of Landslides, Couch Potatoes, and Pocket Tsunamis," p. 31.

31. Sarre, "Calculating the Threat of Tsunami," p. 1.

32. Prager et al., *Furious Earth,* p. 194.

33. Myles, *The Great Waves,* p. 88.

34. Edward Bryant and David Price, "Tsunami Along the South Coast of NSW: The Magnitude and Frequency of Tsunami Along the South Coast of New South Wales, Australia," August 8, 2001. www.uow.edu.au.

35. Bryant and Price, "Tsunami Along the South Coast of NSW."

36. Kerry Sieh and Simon LeVay, *The Earth in Turmoil: Earthquakes, Volcanoes, and Their Impact on Humankind.* New York: W.H. Freeman, 1998, p. 25.

37. Sieh and LeVay, *The Earth in Turmoil,* p. 25.

38. Peter Yanev, "Hokkaido Nansei-oki Earthquake of July 12, 1993," *EQE Review,* Fall 1993. www.eqe.com.

39. Yanev, "Hokkaido Nansei-oki Earthquake of July 12, 1993."

Chapter 4: In the Waves' Wake

40. Georges DeGiorgio, interview with the author, April 2002.

41. Bryant, *Tsunami,* p. 156.

42. Yanev, "Hokkaido Nansei-oki Earthquake of July 12, 1993."

43. Disaster Relief, "Help Arrives in Battered Papua New Guinea," July 21, 1998. www.disasterrelief.org.

44. Quoted in Jennifer Brill, "New Fears of Disease Emerge from Tidal Wave Tragedy," July 24, 1998. www.disaster relief.org.

45. Brian F. Atwater, Marco Cisternos V, Joanne Bourgeois, Walter C. Dudley, James W. Hendley II, and Peter H. Stouffer, *Surviving a Tsunami: Lessons from Chile, Hawaii, and Japan* (Circular 1187). Denver, CO: United States Government Printing Office, 1999, p. 23.

46. DeGiorgio, interview with the author, May 2002.

47. Florida International University, "AMPATH Conference: Tourist Sites in Valdivia," 2002. www.ampath.fiu.edu.

48. Pacific Marine Environmental Laboratory, "Background Paper #3: Land Use Planning," n.d., p. 10. www.pmel. noaa.gov.

Chapter 5: Watching the Waters

49. Smith, "Of Landslides, Couch Potatoes, and Pocket Tsunamis," p. 35.

50. Prager et al., *Furious Earth,* p. 197.

51. International Coordination Group for the Tsunami Warning System in the Pacific, "The Tsunami Warning," September 4, 2001. www.shoa.cl/oceano/itic/itsu.html.

52. Bryant, *Tsunami,* p. 279.

53. Marie C. Eble, "Deep-Ocean Assessment and Reporting of Tsunamis: Background," NOAA—Pacific Marine Environmental Laboratory, n.d. www.pmel.noaa.gov.

54. George Pararas-Carayannis, Patricia Wilson, and Richard Sillcox, *Tsunami Warning!* Honolulu: Intergovernmental

Oceanographic Commission—International Coordinating Group for the Tsunami Warning System in the Pacific, ca. 1995, p. 6.

55. Quoted in Smith, "Of Landslides, Couch Potatoes, and Pocket Tsunamis," p. 35.

56. Quoted in Smith, "Of Landslides, Couch Potatoes, and Pocket Tsunamis," p. 35.

57. Quoted in Todd McLeish, "Tsunami Researcher Makes Big Splash with Landslide Model," *Newswise,* February 1, 2002. www.newswise.com.

58. Quoted in McLeish, "Tsunami Researcher Makes Big Splash with Landslide Model."

59. National Tsunami Hazard Mitigation Program, "Designing for Tsunamis: Seven Principles for Planning and Designing for Tsunami Hazards." Washington, DC: National Tsunami Hazard Mitigation Program, March 2001, p. 1. www.pmel. noaa.gov.

60. Bryant, *Tsunami,* p. 286.

61. Quoted in Andrea Perkins, "Tsunami," *CoastNews: News and Features from San Francisco, the Bay Area, and the North Coast of California,* n.d. www.coastnews.com.

62. Prager et al., *Furious Earth,* p. 216.

Conclusion: Peru, June 23, 2001

63. Lori Dengler, "Impacts of the June 23, 2001 Peru Tsunami," 2001. http://sorrel/humboldt.edu.

64. Dengler, "Impacts of the June 23, 2001 Peru Tsunami."

65. Andrea Munzer, "Relief Work Continues in Quake-Ravaged Peru," July 2, 2001. www.redcross.org.

Glossary

amplitude: The vertical distance of a wave from the bottom of the trough to the top of the crest.

bathymetry: The underwater topography of the seabed floor.

crest: The top of a wave.

depression wave: The leading edge of certain types of tsunamis that causes seawater to recede from the shore before the main waves of the tsunami arrive.

equilibrium: The state and relative level of water at rest (or undisturbed by outside forces).

fault: A fracture in the earth's crust across which there has been relative displacement.

horizontal inundation distance: The maximum distance from the shoreline reached by tsunami waves.

paleotsunami: Prehistoric tsunamis, which are inferred by the geologic record.

period: The amount of time it takes for a crest and a trough of a wave to pass a given location.

plate tectonics: The theory and study of plate formation, movement, interaction, and destruction that attempts to explain earthquakes, volcanoes, mountain building, and other evidence of plate motion.

Richter scale: A scale that allows the amount of energy released by an earthquake to be represented by the numbers 1 to 10.

run-up: The height of a tsunami wave when it comes ashore.

slump: The movement of massive amounts of earth, often underwater, as a result of gravity or of seismic disturbance.

terrestrial: Relating to the land environment.

trench: A deep portion of the ocean floor formed at plate margins where one plate is being subducted beneath another.

trough: The deepest part of a wave.

tsunami: A large and often destructive wave of water formed in response to geologic activity, such as an earthquake, a landslide, or a volcano; also occasionally created through comet or asteroid impact.

tsunamigenic: Any geologic activity that creates tsunamis.

wavelength: The distance between two crests or two troughs of a wave.

wave train: A series of successive waves in a tsunami caused by a single geologic event.

For Further Reading

Author's note: Books that deal with tsunamis exclusively are fairly rare. Tsunamis are often discussed in books that cover other natural phenomena such as earthquakes and volcanoes. Books that reprint highly technical scientific papers are also good sources for tsunami information.

Leslie Allen, Thomas Y. Canby, Ron Fisher, Noel Grove, and Tom Melham, *Raging Forces: Nature in Upheaval.* Washington, DC: National Geographic Society, 1995. Excellent overview of natural disasters. Chapter 2 ("When the Earth Moves") includes tsunamis.

Samantha Bonar, *Tsunamis.* Mankato, MN: Capstone Press, 2001. The author examines why these natural disasters occur, including the role people may play in predicting and surviving tsunamis. The text features a generous use of dates and statistics.

Jon Erickson, *Marine Geology: Undersea Landforms and Life Forms.* New York: Facts On File, 1996. A review of the science of marine geology. Chapters 3 through 6 cover topics related to and including tsunamis, such as plate tectonics, volcanism, and faulting.

Ron Fisher, Tom Melham, Cynthia Russ Ramsay, and Gene S. Stuart, *Nature on the Rampage: Our Violent Earth.* Washington, DC: National Geographic Society, 1986. Many historic disasters are covered in depth. Some classic photographs of tsunamis are included, but the information on research efforts is now somewhat dated.

Christopher Lampton, *Tidal Wave.* Brookfield, CT: Millbrook Press, 1992. Lampton describes some of the most destructive waves of the last century and their effects. He also covers wave generation, causes of tidal waves; plate tectonics, and the tsunami warning system.

Janice McCann and Betsy Shand, *Surviving Natural Disasters: How to Prepare for Earthquakes, Hurricanes, Tornadoes, Floods, Wildfires, Thunderstorms, Blizzards, Tsunamis, Volcanic Eruptions, and Other Calamities.* Salem, OR: Dimi Press, 1995. Excellent to-the-point information on what to do before and after disasters strike.

Lesley Newson, *Devastation! The World's Worst Natural Disasters.* New York: DK Publishing, 1998. Chapter 1 ("Restless Earth") covers volcanoes and earthquakes and the tsunamis in their wake; accompanied by striking photos and helpful world maps with keys to disasters covered in the text.

George Pararas-Carayannis, Patricia Wilson, and Richard Sillcox, *Tsunami Warning!* Honolulu: Intergovernmental Oceanographic Commission—International Coordinating Group for the Tsunami Warning System in the Pacific, ca. 1995. Primarily directed at Hawaiian readers, this richly illustrated book gives straightforward advice about what causes tsunamis and how to survive them.

D.M. Souza, *Powerful Waves.* Minneapolis: Carolrhoda Books, 1992. Interesting information about how tsunamis are formed and a brief look at the science of detecting and warning about them.

Works Consulted

Books

David Alt and Donald W. Hyndman, *Northwest Exposures: A Geologic Story of the Northwest.* Missoula, MT: Mountain Meadow Press, 1995.

Edward Bryant, *Tsunami: The Underrated Hazard.* Cambridge, England: Cambridge University Press, 2001.

Allan Cox, ed., *Plate Tectonics and Geomagnetic Reversals.* San Francisco: W.H. Freeman, 1973.

Walter C. Dudley and Min Lee, *Tsunami!* Honolulu: University of Hawaii Press, 1988.

Richard V. Fisher, Grant Heiken, and Jeffrey B. Hulen, *Volcanoes: Crucibles of Change.* Princeton, NJ: Princeton University Press, 1997.

Ann G. Harris, Esther Tuttle, and Sherwood Tuttle, *Geology of National Parks.* 5th ed. Dubuque, IA: Kendall-Hunt, 1995.

Stephen L. Harris, *Agents of Chaos: Earthquakes, Volcanoes, and Other Natural Disasters.* Missoula, MT: Mountain Presss, 1990.

Barbara H. Keating, Christopher F. Waythomas, and Alastair G. Dawson, eds. *Landslides and Tsunamis.* Basel, Switzerland: Birhauser-Verlag, 2000.

Douglas Myles, *The Great Waves.* New York: McGraw-Hill, 1985.

Plato, *Plato in Twelve Volumes.* Trans. R.G. Bury. 1929. Reprint: Cambridge, MA: Harvard University Press, 1975.

Ellen J. Prager, with Kate Hutton, Costas Synolakis, and Stanley Williams, *Furious Earth: The Science and Nature of Earthquakes, Volcanoes, and Tsunamis.* New York: McGraw-Hill, 2000.

Frank Press and Raymond Siever, *Earth.* 2nd ed. San Francisco: W.H. Freeman, 1978.

Kerry Sieh and Simon LeVay, *The Earth in Turmoil: Earthquakes, Volcanoes, and Their Impact on Humankind.* New York: W.H. Freeman, 1998.

Tom Simkin and Richard S. Fiske, *Krakatau 1883: The Volcanic Eruption and Its Effects.* Washington, DC: Smithsonian Institution Press, 1983.

Periodicals

B.F. Atwater, "Evidence for Great Holocene Earthquakes Along the Outer Coast of Washington State," *Science,* May 22, 1987.

Brian F. Atwater, Marco Cisternos V, Joanne Bourgeois, Walter C. Dudley, James W. Hendley II, and Peter H. Stouffer, *Surviving a Tsunami: Lessons from Chile, Hawaii, and Japan* (Circular 1187). Denver, CO: United States Government Printing Office, 1999.

Edward Bullard, "The Origin of the Oceans," *Scientific American,* September 1969.

Campion Interactive, "Eruption Would Cause Killer Tsunami," *Geographical,* November 2001.

Neal D. Driscoll, Jeffrey K. Weissel, and John D. Goff, "Potential for Large-Scale Submarine Slope Failure and Tsunami Generation Along the U.S. Mid-Atlantic Coast," *Geology,* May 2000.

Gerard Fryer, "The Most Dangerous Wave," *Sciences,* July/August 1995.

Guy Gugliotta, "Huge Asteroid Headed Here—Eventually," *Great Falls Tribune,* April 5, 2002.

J.R. Heirtzler, "Sea-Floor Spreading," *Scientific American,* December 1968.

Patrick M. Hurley, "The Confirmation of Continental Drift," *Scientific American,* April 1968.

Richard A. Kerr, "Faraway Tsunami Hints at a Really Big Northwest Quake," *Science,* February 17, 1995.

Jurgen Kienle, Zygmunt Kowalki, and T.S. Murty, "Tsunami Generated by Eruptions from Mount St. Augustine Volcano, Alaska," *Science,* June 12, 1987.

Scott McCredie, "When Nightmare Waves Appear out of Nowhere to Smash the Land," *Smithsonian,* March 1994.

Richard Monastersky, "Seabed Slide Blamed for Deadly Tsunami," *Science News,* August 14, 1999.

———, "Waves of Death: Why the New Guinea Tsunami Carries Bad News for North America," *Science News,* October 3, 1998.

Douglas L. Smith, "Of Landslides, Couch Potatoes, and Pocket Tsunamis," *Engineering & Science*, no. 1, 2000.

Internet Sources

Australian Broadcasting Corporation Online, "Transcript, Links, and Further Information for 'Tsunami,'" n.d. www.abc.net.au.

Jennifer Brill, "New Fears of Disease Emerge from Tidal Wave Tragedy," July 24, 1998. www.disasterrelief.org.

Kathryn Brown, "Tsunami? At Lake Tahoe? Surprised Tourists Could Catch the Ultimate Wave," June 10, 2000. www.science news.org.

Edward Bryant, University of Wollongong School of Geosciences, "Questions and Answers on Current Topics in Geosciences," August 12, 1999. www.uow.edu.au.

Edward Bryant and David Price, "Tsunami Along the South Coast of NSW: The Magnitude and Frequency of Tsunami Along the South Coast of New South Wales, Australia," August 8, 2001. www.uow.edu.au.

Ciudad de Valdivia, "Valdivia Chile por Antipodas," 2001. www.valdiviachile.cl.

CNN.com, "Taiwan Braces for Quake Aftershocks," April 1, 2002. www.cnn.com.

Leonard David, "Asteroid Busting: We Have the Technology," Space.com, May 31, 2001. www.space.com.

Lori Dengler, "Impacts of the June 23, 2001 Peru Tsunami," 2001. http://sorrel/humboldt.edu.

Disaster Relief, "Help Arrives in Battered Papua New Guinea," July 21, 1998. www.disasterrelief.org.

Marie C. Eble, "Deep-Ocean Assessment and Reporting of Tsunamis: Background," NOAA—Pacific Marine Environmental Laboratory, n.d. www.pmel.noaa.gov.

Extreme Science, "Biggest Wave: Lituya Bay Tsunami," 2002. www.extremescience.com.

Florida International University, "AMPATH Conference: Tourist Sites in Valdivia," 2002. www.ampath.fiu.edu.

Eric L. Geist, "Local Tsunamis in the Pacific Northwest," U.S. Geological Survey—Western Region Coastal and Marine Geology, June 28, 1999. http://walrus.wr.usgs.gov.

———, "Tsunamis and Earthquakes," August 3, 2001. http://walrus.wr.usgs.gov.

Jana Goldman, "NOAA to Participate in Tsunami Review, International Symposium," August 6, 2001. www.publicaffairs.noaa.gov.

International Coordination Group for the Tsunami Warning System in the Pacific, "The Tsunami Warning," September 4, 2001. www.shoa.cl/oceano/itic/itsu.html.

Bruce Jaffe, Guy Gelfenbaum, and Robert Peters, "Preliminary Analysis of Sedimentary Deposits from the June 23, 2001 Peru Tsunami: The Importance of Studying Tsunami Sediments," USGS—Western Region Coastal Marine Geology Program, January 24, 2002. http://walrus.wr.usgs.gov.

"Killer Wave, July 20, 1998," *The News Hour with Jim Lehrer.* www.pbs.org.

King County Office of Emergency Management, Emergency Management Division, Department of Information and

Administrative Services, "Tsunamis and Seiches," part 1, September 24, 1998. www.metrokc.gov.

Stephanie Kriner, "Seafloor Landslide Could Push Tsunami Toward U.S. East Coast," May 2000. www.disasterrelief.org.

Todd McLeish, "Tsunami Researcher Makes Big Splash with Landslide Model," *Newswise,* February 1, 2002. www.news wise.com.

K. Meguro, "Okushiri Island: Two Years After the Earthquake," International Center for Disaster—Mitigation Engineering Institute of Industrial Science, University of Tokyo, July–September 1995. http://incede.iis.u-tokyo.ac.jp.

Andrea Munzer, "Relief Work Continues in Quake-Ravaged Peru," July 2, 2001. www.redcross.org.

National Oceanographic and Atmospheric Administration/ National Weather Service, "International Tsunami Information Center," n.d. http://205.156.54.206/pr/itic/.

National Science Foundation, "NSF Award Abstracts— #0086571: Upgrading Oregon State's Multidirectional Wave Basin for Remote Tsunami Research," January 3, 2002. www.fastlane.nsf.gov.

National Tsunami Hazard Mitigation Program, "Designing for Tsunamis: Seven Principles for Planning and Designing for Tsunami Hazards." Washington, DC: National Tsunami Hazard Mitigation Program, March 2001. www.pmel.noaa.gov.

NOAA Public Affairs, "NOAA and Tsunamis," January 2002. www.publicaffairs.noaa. gov.

Oregon State University, O.H. Hinsdale Wave Research Laboratory, "Directional Wave Basin," November 14, 2000. www.ccee.orst.edu.

Pacific Marine Environmental Laboratory, "Background Paper #3: Land Use Planning," n.d. www.pmel.noaa.gov.

Daniel Pendick, "Savage Earth. Waves of Destruction: Tsunamis," PBS Online/WNET Thirteen New York, n.d. www.pbs.org.

Andrea Perkins, "Tsunami," *CoastNews: News and Features from San Francisco, the Bay Area, and the North Coast of California,* n.d. www.coastnews.com.

Alan Ruffman, "Tsunami Runup Mapping as an Emergency Preparedness Planning Tool: The 1929 Tsunami in St. Lawrence, Newfoundland," Geomarine Associates Contract Report for Emergency Preparedness Canada, Directorate of Research and Development, 1996. www.epc-pcc.gc.ca.

Alastair Sarre, "Calculating the Threat of Tsunami," *NOVA: Science in the News,* Australian Foundation for Science. www.science.org.au.

Thomas J. Sokolowski, "West Coast and Alaska Tsunami Warning Center: Mission and Overview," November 2, 2001. http://wcatwc.gov.

Tim Thwaites, "Modelling Tsunami Waves," *Monash Magazine,* February 1998. www.monash.edu.au.

Lyn Topinka, "Eruption Summary—May 18, 1980 Eruption of Mount St. Helens," U.S. Geological Survey/Cascades Volcano Observatory, August 8, 2000. http://vulcan.wr.usgs.gov.

University of Southern California Tsunami Research Group, "Papua New Guinea July 31–August 8, 1998," August 10, 1998. www.usc.edu.

U.S. Geological Survey—Western Region Coastal and Marine Geology, "Life of a Tsunami," June 28, 1999. http://walrus.wr.usgs.gov.

V.I. Usov, "Data Catalogue for Near-Source Tsunami Observed in Kuril Isls. and Sakhalin Is.," Sakhalin Tsunami Warning Center, April 10, 1998. www.science.sakhalin.ru.

West Coast & Alaska Tsunami Warning Center, "Tsunami of 23 June 2001," 2001. http://wcatwc.gov.

———, "TsunamiReady," May 6, 2002. http://wcatwc.gov.

Wycliffe International, "Swept Away: Surprising Hope in the Wake of a Tragic Tsunami," Fall 2001. http://www.wycliffe.org.

Peter Yanev, "Hokkaido Nansei-oki Earthquake of July 12, 1993," *EQE Review,* Fall 1993. www.eqe.com.

Websites

Australian Academy of Science (www.science.org.au). The Australian Academy of Science maintains an extremely informative set of pages, starting with "Calculating the Threat of Tsunami."

EarthNet, "From Puzzle to Theory: Plate Tectonics" This is a good introduction to the theory that revolutionized geology.

Earthquake News (www.earthquakenews.com). Earthquake News has up-to-the-minute stories about daily earthquake activity from around the world. This site serves as a good starting point for investigating possible tsunamigenic activity.

ExploreZone.com, "Tsunamiscience" (http://explorezone.com.). This site contains basic information and informative animations, as well as helpful links to other sites.

Extreme Science, "Biggest Wave: Lituya Bay Tsunami" (www.extremescience.com.). A brief look at the largest recorded wave in history. There is some debate over whether or not this was a tsunami, but the event remains fascinating.

Federal Emergency Management Agency, "Backgrounder: Tsunami" (www.fema.gov.). Basic information about causes of tsunamis and some "Did You Know?" fun facts.

National Oceanographic and Atmospheric Admnistration (www.nws.noaa.gov.). This informative website includes tsunami causes, safety information, and very interesting photographs.

NOAA's International Tsunami Information Center (http://205.156.54.206/pr/itic). This website has links to current tsunami events, research efforts, safety rules, and further reading sources.

NOAA's West Coast and Alaska Tsunami Warning Center (http://wcatwc.gov). This includes links to tide gauges and a page of the most recent tsunamis; also has interesting information about the "TsunamiReady" community program.

Pacific Marine Environmental Laboratory (www.pmel. noaa.gov). This branch of NOAA maintains a comprehensive tsunami site. The frequently asked questions page is particularly informative.

University of Southern California's Tsunami Research Group (www.usc.edu). This website of a cutting-edge research department includes results from field surveys as well as computer animation of future potential tsunamis.

University of Washington, Geophysics Department, *"Tsunami!"* (www.geophys.washington.edu). The site has useful information about tsunami causes, warning systems, and historic tsunamis.

Index

Picture Credits

About the Author

Andrew A. Kling became fascinated with earth sciences at a young age. His middle school science teacher introduced him to plate tectonics, which suddenly helped explain all the geologic phenomena about which he'd learned. He earned a bachelor's degree in geology as a result of this interest.

During fifteen years as a National Park Service ranger, Kling developed and facilitated public programs about geologic and other natural science topics, including earthquakes and weather phenomena. From 1996 to 1999, he served as writer and editor for the Cape Hatteras National Seashore newspaper and planned and implemented the visitor and public information services programs during the relocation of the Cape Hatteras Lighthouse. For the National Park Service, he cowrote *Sea, Sands, and Sounds: A Guide to Barrier Island Ecology and Geology,* a curriculum guide for middle school educators.

Kling currently lives in Montana, working as a freelance writer, editor, interpretive media developer, and consultant.